# The Master Jesus Speaks

## bj King

1st WORLD
PUBLISHING

The Master Jesus Speaks

bj King

Copyright © 2025 by bj King

Published by 1st World Publishing
P.O. Box 2211, Fairfield, Iowa 52556
tel: 641-209-5000 • fax: 866-440-5234
web: www.1stworldpublishing.com

First Edition

ISBN Softcover: 978-1-4218-3583-9

LCCN: Library of Congress Cataloging-in-Publication Data

This material has been written and published for educational purposes to enhance one's well-being. In regard to health issues, the information is not intended as a substitute for appropriate care and advice from health professionals, nor does it equate to the assumption of medical or any other form of liability on the part of the publisher or author. The publisher and author shall have neither liability nor responsibility to any person or entity with respect to loss, damages, or injury claimed to be caused directly or indirectly by any information in this book.

# Table of Contents

"Please stop using the crucifix cross to represent Me. I am not dead. I ascended and am still alive working and growing and available to you. Please use the even Maltese cross to represent Me, it represents balance of male and female energies and living a balanced life."

1.

# Jesus Speaks Today

The first time I personally encountered Jesus was September 30, 1982. I was unemployed from a bank consulting job that had just ended. I went to a bookstore to look for a book on how to find my life's purpose. I looked in the self-help, psychology and religion sections. Disappointed at not finding what I thought I needed; I began to walk away. Suddenly as I passed the occult section, which as a Christian I would normally avoid, a book flew off the top shelf and landed on the floor in front of me. The name of the book was *Psychic Energy*. The book did not aesthetically appeal to me, but the circumstances of it flying through the air caused me to purchase it, against my better judgment. On the drive home from the bookstore I made an agreement with God that I would only open the book to one page, like we used to do with the Bible, when we sought answers. I would close my eyes and open this book and expect whatever God wanted to tell me would be on one page.

On the drive home from the bookstore I made an agreement with God that I would only open the book to one page, like we used to do the *Bible*, when we sought answers. I would close my eyes and open this book and expect whatever God wanted to tell me would be on one page.

That's what I did and the page I opened to was a meditation to receive inspired writing from my soul. I had never meditated. As the book suggested I took a shower, put on a loose fitting robe, took the phone off the hook and sat on the couch with my spine straight and a pen and legal pad on my lap. The words began to appear telepathically, not a voice, just words, on the right side of my brain as soon as I counted down the way the book suggested. The information I received filled seven legal sized pages. I was told I would no longer be a bank teller I Was to become an artist and a writer.

Since that day I have followed the guidance that comes to me through my meditations. The next time Jesus appeared to me was one morning when I awakened from sleep and the shape of His image in light was standing at the foot of my bed. He asked me to start a non-profit spiritual retreat organization. He asked me to call it Namaste, which I did.

He came in 1998 and asked me to channel the information about the 49 Rays of God, which took me three years, because it is so complex. This information is available as an app for your phone through Amazon.

He came in 2003 and asked me to start a Mystery School which was to be called the Namaste Mystery School of Remembering and said the Spiritual Hierarchy Masters would channel the information to publish each month. I did this from 2003-2025. There are now 217 lessons about spiritual subjects.

More recently he came and asked me to channel and write His desires for Humanity. These are the messages I will share with you.

# 2.

# Jesus Speaks of Our Future

"There are no endings in Spirit. I am still growing and learning even as you are, for all life expands in the endless creation of God's nature. Growth is the only evidence life exists. You constantly choose spiritual life or death by your willingness to transform your limited consciousness into the grace of a broader reality. To assist with the greater transformation in Humanity's reality, I hope the offerings of truth I have brought will support your desire to become more peaceful, loving and joyful as you go toward your heritage with certainty and true companionship.

"I hope by identifying those errors of past thinking and showing you the promise of a new day, we now hold a common understanding from my heart to yours. Let me highlight once more what I wish you to know and share with others.

a. "Live every day, use every thought as if it were your last. Leave no kind action or peaceful thought unexpressed.

b. "Meditate daily and listen unceasingly so that, through the Holy Power granted to your soul by our Creator, you will know the actions you should take each day. In your jargon, stay tuned in. That way you will never be afraid or wonder what is going to happen. You will be told, as the elect of higher consciousness, what you are to accomplish, and with whom you will be working. A weekly meditation with others is also necessary, for these groups of Light Workers sitting together will make the task of your continuous communication easier and more supportive. Moreover, your own body will begin to glow from this increased energy amplification. It aids your own enlightenment or return to God identity.

c. "Join with others to influence your national and international governments to embody the ideal of peace in all that they do and intend. Spiritual people often ignore the everyday responsibilities of citizenship. But this must change. It will take every loving person on the planet to swell the voice that speaks to government. Do all you legally can to demand peace at every level of life.

"I affirm: if you do these things, and do them willingly, with dedication and determination, you will likely be among the Golden Age dwellers on the planet Earth during the thousand years following the Earth's cleansing. This will be a time of great opportunity and joy, and I pray all will hear the call of their inner voice as it tugs their hearts, reminding them to answer their Creator's call, if they have not already done so. Do this in remembrance of God and of all the religious of this Earth, and we will one day stand together in the great festivity of joy that is yet coming for those of pure mind and heart, as demonstrated through everyday action and behavior.

"Christians, please give up your complacency and self-righteousness that Jesus is your savior and you need to do nothing more. Right actions balance out past negativity and regrettable deeds, and teach you usefulness and service much needed in the galaxy.

"I tell you, I can save no one who will not change. Moreover, I can save no one who clings to past memories of me as if they were today's truth. Only your own thoughts and actions can save you. Jesus as I was in biblical times has changed, grown. I know more than I did then, but the message is the same now as it was then: LOVE GOD! You must acknowledge that a Force greater than all your bombs put together has an energy system to rotate your planet daily in a cradle of rhythm and harmony. Honor the Force which brings you into contact with both Sun and Moon, and the starlit heavens of your own 12th Universe.

"It is time to say it again so there is no misunderstanding. The majority of people on Earth are spiritually lazy and have allowed a few minds to conceive of evil beyond description. Further, you have allowed a small number of maniacs to guide your destiny and to bring you to the possibility of nuclear destruction from which your physical body will not survive. You are committing cultural suicide by your own indifference to the few who take power and rush blindly into technological doom.

"Can you perceive this from your TV news programs, the radio, and your newspapers? Have you no sense of what you are allowing to happen?

"Now let me be a true brother to you and a World Teacher who would have no one lost. Peace is a choice. War is a choice. Your Human consciousness is choosing the path of physical demolition. Unless you begin at once to cooperate, I cannot save your body, nor will God, for you have Freewill to create your own world and live out what you have created. God has little to do with the conditions on your planet. You have brought them to you by your thoughts, actions and desires.

"You live in a World of matter where the events happen through your own past and present volition. Therefore, by your Freewill, look to see what you would have. And if you do not like the present train of events that bring me from the Creator to clarify your position, then it is you who must change them.

"I will do all I can to assist, for there is a small core of spiritual Light Bearers already on Earth trying desperately to turn the tide of darkness and to reach those uncommitted souls who tranquilize their way into emotional denial. Using a vast array of escape activities such as alcohol, drugs, food, TV and other pursuits to ignore the present danger and responsibility to do something about it, the mass of Humanity still lies asleep. It must be awakened.

"I brought you grace 2,000 years ago. I guaranteed that if you were willing to return to Spirit of the Christ, which is eternal truth, and if you would set a personal example, not of self-righteousness, but of unconditional love and caring, then I could assist and help. I will if you agree to do your part.

"Because of the plans our Creator intends for this planet, we have only a short time to create a more peaceful and harmonious Earth. For the black blanket of egocentricity and irresponsibility chokes the Earth upon which you walk. Wake up and come into the Light where you belong, and where your Creator would have you be. State your preference and live its tenets. The balance of energies is so critical at this time that the immense rescue team we are using to send out huge amounts of light will fail if you do not respond.

"It is to you, my Light Bearers, that we pass the wand of power and encouragement. You are the leaders of the New Age and a new civilization. Proclaim the truth of love, be the Love as a model for those who cannot understand. This is your true calling, to be the Light, to be the love, to stand, as once I did, in spreading the word of love to the minds of all children, men and women.

"Since no stone will be left unturned by those of us in the heavenly realms to awaken all of Humanity in this critical moment, we need every soul to remember its true nature and take command of this planet in the name of peace. We need earthly angels to practice the truth of mind and heart. We need a savior, and the savior is you collectively. Together you are the savior, and this is your most opportune hour. Behave like the savior now, for the stage is set and the cast is called. Your planetary play is in the third act where the forces of good and evil have been long battling, and for the moment it looks as if the good force is not doing well. Yet, help can come to reverse the situation if you will but create it by meditation and follow it with heartfelt action.

"Mother Earth, your heroine, awaits Humanity's support as Her hero in this drama, and Her hero is all of you collectively. The problem has been Humankind, and the answer is Humankind. You are both villain and hero. End this duality and speak your last lines. It is the hero's role to take the final bow and to receive approbation in a garland of spiritual appreciation, acclaim and applause.

"We, your audience of heavenly hosts, will walk forward with you as your last act in the drama is called, sending mighty streams of energy to back your motives. Before the curtain comes down, let us march into the light with heads held high, hearts infused with love, and peace our only goal. Earth will, Herself, be rescued and kept alive no matter what happens, but those beings of hatred and war will not remain here spiritually to see the planet's future adventure.

"I, the one called Jesus in the olden times, am with you ever anew in your present situation and in your present plight. This is a spiritual showdown, a time of separating those who love God and those who do not.

"Joining with others in small groups increases the light of your aura, or energy field. But in addition, you will have a sense of community, a community which may not be composed of your blood relatives or usual circle of friends. You may even find that your new spiritual family becomes very dear to you in a short time because these beings match your soul vibration, and the bonding which you can feel with them may exceed that of the usual love relationship you are used to having with family and friends.

"Like attracts Like. This is the Law of the Universe. As you raise your energies through daily meditations and by sharing this greater awareness with others, you will reach higher and higher realms of soul communication, and possibly mental telepathy with those like myself who await your increased ability to form the communication link, the system of contact with goodness wherever it resides.

"The Golden Age of which I have spoken is the time when the usual solidity of things on Earth must change. What has been invisible for thousands of years in Spirit, or as Heaven, will become increasingly real to you. Your usual physical senses will be expanded and will flow into awareness of things unseen, things you previously could not imagine or reach.

"The ability to flow even deeper into spiritual awareness may seem strange to you at first, but I assure you, beloveds, that it is necessary and will quickly become your usual way of behaving in this world. Remember, I said you should be in this World, but not of it? This was my meaning. You are here in a physical body, but you need not be weighed down by its mere physical senses. You will be gaining higher senses of knowing, hearing and seeing what Humankind has lost during the past eons of descent into lower and lower vibrations in the material world. To know directly from the cosmic realms is the greatest experience of all, and many will achieve this sensitive, intuitive state.

"Without daily contact, the new communication pathways cannot be built, and the personality will be left in darkness when others will be leaping forward in their ability to intuit and know the Will of God by Soul Guidance. Your meditation times will build this communication link of Light and higher energy vibration which can never fail you once the link is forged.

"Contact your own internal spiritual teacher and your soul, who can then act like a gigantic switchboard to keep you in touch with the unseen beings like myself. Remember, you must build this communication system from Earth to us. We can provide the plan, but you must choose and carry it into fruition. This is the only way you can be 'saved' or born into the Kingdom of God. Become what God envisions for you.

"When enough of you Light Workers have joined together to unify the positive love force on the planet, much will be possible in the realm of mind where all creation begins. Here, where the energy blueprint of manifestation is formed, one and one equal a sum greater than two. And when two or more are gathered in conviction and agreement, that creative power increases by an exponential magnitude that your mathematics cannot really express. By thought alone, by pure intention and feeling, does creation cast a pattern onto the etheric life web which holds space together. Here, in that tiny web of refined subatomic structures, which your instruments yet fail to totally expose, does infinity coax finite reality into form.

"Only through love can one grasp a hint of how life began and how it continually expands beyond itself, ever growing and flowing in pure joy. Today's churches must change. They have deified me instead of encouraging each child of God to go into his/her own inner soul sanctuary and bring forth God's empowering energy, which could be then joined in concert with others of like intention. Today, I advise you that any church official who does not drop meaningless ritual and lead its members to quiet times with their souls must face the effect of this behavior.

"By meditating, you can live God's commandments more easily, especially, love God, love God with all your heart, mind and soul, and your brothers and sisters as yourself. I call forth the Holy God Power within you to hear my messages and bring you into the Golden Age as a bright and shining example of the new life all can have through willingness to accept the love we offer.

"Remarks such as 'I don't have time' or 'I'm too busy' are merely the workings of your egotistical personality, which keeps you in a place of separation from the Creator, from Heaven. I assure you, if you meet us halfway, your destiny as Light Workers in the Golden Age ahead is affirmed. But I cannot save you from your lower self, that limited part which prevents your greater good. If you are willing to learn and to serve, then you will be welcomed to join us in Heaven.

"This is Earth's time of transformation. This is the time when the Creator has required that there must be peace. Without peace, the Earth will be in pain and chaos. I do not seek to frighten you or make you fearful for your body. Those of you who believe in God and the lesson of resurrection which I brought to Humanity 2,000 years ago will understand the loss of your body is not the vital issue, anyway. The condition of your soul is. The present situation is critical.

"In times past, when Humankind perpetrated destructive acts, the planet had to be cleansed in order for a fresh start to occur. It is this experience you are about to face. There has been so much hatred, so much war, and recent invasions of space that another cleansing time will occur on the Earth unless Humanity does a rapid reverse to peace, and only peace.

"This time, known as the Tribulation, is upon you and upon the planet now, and this is a last, urgent call to all of you to wake up, accept your soul responsibilities, and demonstrate peaceful thoughts and reactions. Be sure you stay in contact with your soul. You are the savior of Humankind, and it is only through your efforts at this hour that Earth can be saved.

"If Earth changes are required, only those who are of the higher consciousness will be brought back for the thousand years of peace. As the ignorant Humans, those who ignore the truth and leave the planet, their souls will be relocated to planets of a lower vibration than Earth, to Ploarus or Octegon. We wish to dispel these aggressive thoughts that have accumulated in the band of invisible light around your spinning spaceship Earth. Anyone who chooses to awaken can still do so with the least possible pain and suffering.

"Know that I am joined in this project by the teachers of all times and places: Buddha, Moses, Krishna and Mohammed, and thousands of others from our Universe who stand together to provide the support the planet needs. Our present efforts on Humanity's behalf cannot be continued with this intense priority indefinitely. There are other activities in the Universe which demand our energiesand attention. We will never leave you comfortless, but this is the time to take advantage of God's unprecedented special aid to Earth.

"Because of your Freewill, you have the ability to do what you will, but that freedom has been your nemesis. Therefore, I urge you to quell your doubting minds and selfish personalities and place your attention only on what is reverent and peaceful at every level of life. Whether you call yourself agnostic, or are a member of some religious body, is not the issue. The issue is your demonstration that you love God, love peace.

"Many are called, but few will answer. This is the result of Humanity's stubborn, unrelenting insistence on doing things his/her own way. I ask you, has this brought you the World of peace and love and joy which you desire? God is breathing, or extending out, and then will breathe us all Home again to enjoy our spiritual future. There is a plan of great promise and joy for all who choose it. Trust and believe.

"Even if the majority will lazily ignore the summons, and an active portion seize war as their mode of life, the New Age will be in full force by the turn of the century. Your three choices today are whether you wish to learn and serve now, or later, under pain and suffering caused by spiritual procrastination, or not at all. I recommend you step forward to your destiny in the Light now where you will go forward with mighty companions in Spirit, for we in the greater realms truly love you and desire only your good.

"God is with you, children of creation and souls of an expanding tomorrow. We have gone to prepare a place for you, but it is your own will, your choice, which determines your rank henceforth. All is prepared for the magnificent band of Light Workers to join together under direct revelation. However, only your commitment will bring the power into and through you for your own advancement and for service to Humanity.

"I, the Christ, World Teacher, do hereby call forward any sincere person on planet Earth to become a lover of God, a lover of planet Earth, a lover of yourself and all living things throughout the Omniverse. This planet needs you to volunteer to offer love and peace to all. By the power and authority of my role as your World Teacher, I do grant you the full support of Heaven in your responsibilities as envoys of World and Universal peace. Know that you are, henceforth, never alone, and that an additional personal guide or teacher will be provided to you when your meditative communication system is linked to Heaven.

"My greatest role is that of being the Gold Ray to all the Universes. Nevertheless, I attend your planet now in this critical hour, and am joined here by a mighty cosmic companion called the Silver Ray. The Silver Ray is the second creation of God, Who has created all other Rays except myself, and brings Earth both the color spectrum of the rainbow and the glowing nighttime reminder of God, your moonlight.

"The Silver Ray, the Great Ray of Hope and Healing, has volunteered to ease the subconscious pain and the soul memories of your eight-million-year-long negative experiences so that there will be peace on Earth at last. You will hear this great, yet gentle, healing energy call you forth to revere God and all of life. "

# 3.

# The Master Jesus Speaks

"At this critical period of planetary transition into a new Cosmic Age, the Age of Aquarius, it is mandatory that Humanity be liberated from lack of Spiritual Truth. The New Age will involve a new World, a new civilization, as has been prophesied. You've heard it referred to as a 'new heaven and new Earth.' Humans must become knowledgeable of their true identity as aspects of God, as infinite and immortal Spiritual Beings. I AM coming forth to speak of Spiritual Truth".

# 4.

# Rings Around Earth

"January 20, 1920, the Spiritual Hierarchy created and positioned a series of electromagnetic Rings around the Earth three miles outside Earth's atmosphere. The purpose of the Rings is to hold ideas, inspirations and information that aware Humans can access during altered states of consciousness and utilize them to further evolution. These ideas and images are added to the Rings on a regular basis. Their purpose is to make available inventions, artistic images, music, healing techniques, formulas and methods of surgery to inspire evolution for the Aquarian Age.

"Everything is composed of energy. What exists around and on the Earth has been changed, destroyed or buried by great earthquakes, flood, land-slides, sunken continents (such as Atlantis and Mu), plus the catastrophic tipping of Earth's axis during the Pleistocene Epoch about 4 million years ago, resulting in the 'ice ages.'

"This present World will be transformed energetically and new planetary conditions in the Fourth dimension will prevail on Earth. The new race of Humans in this Age will express a different quality of consciousness, a Fourth dimensional consciousness and have abilities considered Super-Human in today's World. "

"This can only unfold if Humans are finally exposed to the truth about who they are and the truth about the Earth, Solar System, Universe, Omniverse, the Spiritual Hierarchy, Angels and the Great White Brotherhood. Also, the truth of why I came to Earth, not to relieve the sins of Humanity, but to prove ascension and to anchor the energies of the Cosmic Christ Consciousness.

"Without adequate knowledge of Spiritual Realms of Life and authentic and true information regarding Human's ultimate destiny beyond the

Human plane, Humanity cannot wake up to the truth. Spiritual Teachings and Revelations have been offered to Humanity throughout the Ages, and many of these teachings still exist, referred to as scriptures. These teachings and revelations were written in ancient or now dead languages and have been mistranslated or purposely distorted by unscrupulous authorities to increase their prestige and power. This was also done deliberately to confuse and control Humans for the benefit of Church and political leaders. True religion has been stripped of its Spirituality to become a dogma of literal words, pretentious rituals and hallowed traditions.

"True spiritual teaching has not been offered to Humanity in centuries. The word 'shenah' described and related to conditions and time-periods of Human history in the original Chaldean writings are correctly defined to mean 'sleep; dream; changes.' The Old Testament writers of Humanity's origins mistranslated the ancient Chaldean word 'shenah' as 'years.'

"Due to this kind of mistranslation, biblical scholars and clerics have been relating Human's arrival on Earth as beginning some 8,000 years ago. However, the 'years' they related to Adam, Seth, Enos, Cainan, Mahalaleel, Jared, Enoch, Methuselah, Lamech and Noah had each covered long periods of great changes and mutations on Earth, actually involving many Cosmic Ages and Cycles. These biblical names not only represent, in some cases, important Spiritual Beings, but also relate to and describe the quality of Humanity's mass consciousness and its various civilizations that existed during those periods.

"The *Bible* or adaptations of the King James version of the *Bible* refer to Jehovah and Yahweh as if they were the Creator God of all Universes, which they were not. They were lesser beings holding authority during those periods of history. This 'mistranslation' corrected, in itself, should change Christian belief, as well as the true purpose of my coming to Earth as a Human.

"Due to mistranslations of the *Bible*, neither Christianity nor Judaism relates Human souls as aspects of God. Neither admits the divinity contained within each Human. "

"The single most important thing a Human can do is realize their true identity as an aspect of God, a spirit being. "

"The Judaic-Christian *Bible*, though originally written by various Humans and then translated into different languages by other Humans, is yet believed by many religionists as being the pure 'Word of God.' Regardless of probable mistranslations by various scribes, priests, translators and theologians over the centuries, the *Bible* is revered to a greater extent than any more direct Spiritual Teaching or Revelation from God. Unfortunately, most Humans believe God quit speaking directly with Humans centuries ago, which is not true. Translating languages into English can be unclear, because certain words were then and can now be defined in many ways. Also, the number of times the *Bible* has been revised and translated tends to have distorted the original meaning of my message.

"If one considers the *Bible* to be the actual 'Word of God,' it should be realized that much of the Old Testament merely describes historical experiences of the Jewish people and that the New Testament contains various activities attributed to me and my disciples and is not the Word of God. You and I have already discussed the mistranslation of the Beatitudes, which I corrected my true meaning through you several years ago. I think it wise to mention those corrections here. "

"I taught using parables, because that is where the level of Human consciousness was at that time in history. I concerned myself with teaching general principles, which had to do with mental states. As a person thinks, so they will become. "

# 5.

# Jesus's Revised Beatitudes

Matthew 5:1 from the King James Version:

"Blessed are the poor in spirit: for theirs is the kingdom of heaven."

"The word 'poor' could mean impoverished, depleted, lacking in ability, absent of quality, low in potential, or deficient. It can also mean 'simple.' My reference was to 'simplicity.' I was encouraging the people to refrain from complex rituals and creating spiritual hierarchies. I taught there is only one Spirit and that Spirit is within us and within all things. Connecting to that Spirit is a simple process and does not require structure, permission, intermediaries, prerequisites or process. It requires silence, intention, acceptance, Love and simplicity.

"Blessed are they that mourn: for they shall be comforted."

"In Aramaic, "mourning" could mean sorrow, grief, pain, or regret. Humans always have the choice of learning by spiritual unfoldment or by painful experience. Most people do not seek God whole-heartedly unless trouble, sorrow or failure appears in their lives. I was referring to the 'value of mourning' as in 'the act of purging and releasing'. When a person first experiences loss, whether this is through the death of a loved one, the death of a marriage, loss of health, loss of a career or job, loss of home, or loss of financial or social position, the first reaction is shock, depression and/or grief. When the shock passes and a person accepts the circumstance and releases what has been, they open a space for the new that can come. Grieving is clinging to – mourning is letting go, releasing, purging, which allows the emergence, the comfort of a new stage of life. Often in retrospect we can see the loss was a blessing in disguise.

<u>"Blessed are the meek, for they shall inherit the Earth."</u>

"In Aramaic the word 'meek' could mean humble, poor, subservient, lacking self respect, or self-effacing. None of these are the meaning I intended in using the word. My meaning was 'moderation, equilibrium, balance'. In balance there is wholeness, fulfillment and blessing. There is no need to hoard. If hoarding ceased, there would be plenty of all for all. Humans never truly own anything; they are only stewards. They are most happy and fulfilled when they are steward-shipping only what they truly love. 'Meek' can also mean 'open to the will of God,' which is a mental attitude that draws prosperity to an individual.

"The word 'Earth' does not refer merely to the terrestrial globe of Earth. Earth in this context I meant 'manifestation or abundance.' Manifestation is the result of cause. Causation is mental. By 'Earth' I meant the whole of your outer experience. By 'to inherit the Earth' I meant to have dominion over your outer experience through thought. If you live in balance and moderation, with lovingly directed thoughts you will manifest the life your heart desires, because you are open to the will of God for your lives. God's will for your lives is joy, love, abundance and perfect health.

<u>"Blessed are those who hunger and thirst after righteousness; for they shall be filled."</u>

"'Righteousness' does not refer just to right conduct, but also to right thinking in all areas of your lives. Right thinking is the only thing that will produce desired results. Righteousness can also mean harmonious thoughts. If you seek to be in harmony with your thoughts, the results will be a harmonious, fulfilling life. To 'hunger and thirst' refers to praying constantly for wisdom and guidance.

'Righteousness' means being right in your heart. Through the heart you feel the Presence of your Creator. The heart is a powerful magnet, which generates life energy and draws to you all you need and desire."

"Blessed are the merciful for they shall receive mercy."

"If you extend mercy, you will receive mercy. What matters most is that you be merciful in your thinking. If you commit kind deeds out of fear or in order to receive rewards, or the good opinion or favor of others, you are being hypocritical and your rewards will be as tainted as your motive.

"Blessed are the pure in heart: for they shall see God."

"God has no physical form, other than as everything and everyone around you and yourselves. To 'see', in this sense, means to receive spiritual perception, spiritual sight; the sight that causes you to actually see everything and everyone as an aspect of God. To 'see' God is to understand the truth of unity, all as One. 'Purity' is to understand God as the only real Cause; the only real Power. I could have said, blessed are they who recognize God as the only real Cause and Presence, not just in theory but practically, in every thought and area of their lives.

"The word 'heart' in the *Bible* can also refer to the subconscious mind. Head knowledge is learned expression. Heart knowledge is that which you live and actualize. You are called to re-educate the subconscious by practicing the Presence of God at all times in all circumstances. To be 'pure in heart' is to have 'innocent perception,' to recognize that everything was created in innocence. "

"Blessed are the peacemakers: for they shall be called the children of God."

"To become 'peacemakers' is to recognize the Oneness of Spirit and to implement that recognition in your thoughts and actions; to rise above a dualistic approach to living. You normally see life as a conflict between polar opposites. It is your challenge to end dualistic thinking. In the word 'peacemaker' I AM not referring to your being diplomats, negotiators, counselors or ministers; as in the settling of disputes. I AM referring rather to seeking to perceive wholeness in all things; to end separation and duality. You have been conditioned by the presence of what appears to be opposites: up/down, male/female, in/out, forward/backward, black/white, happy/sad, light/dark. You are called to rise above viewing life as a conflict between these seeming opposites.

"Light and dark are not opposites, but represent variable conditions of exposure to light sources. Males and females both contain male and female hormones and attributes. Each seeming opposite is a percentage of the Presence of the whole.

"You have thus far seen the process of creating energy as a result of polar resistive, friction-generated process. You are to move to see the possibility of magnetism – the space between the seeming opposites as your source of energy. You have the potential to end conflict and to create what seems to be free energy. You often create problems or conflicts for yourselves so you can feel smart, intelligent, accomplished when you resolve them. "

"Blessed are they that are persecuted for righteousness' sake: for theirs is the kingdom of heaven."

"When you reach a point where you can consciously 'be' the love that you are, know you are an aspect of God (Love), you are empowered to transcend suffering or illusions. Through love you have power over any situation, but to prove this to yourselves, to really 'know' it, you must set yourselves up to overcome adversity through the power of love.

"God=Love. When you know and completely understand this truth, illusions, adversities and hardships will cease to exist in your lives.

"There is no virtue in martyrdom. There is no virtue or advantage in being persecuted or annoyed by other people. This cannot happen unless there is something within you; still, that matches this energetically. You will be treated as you expect to be treated, but this expectation must be backed by truth. What you see and experience at any time is your own concept of reality. You create the potential for hindrance and persecution by what you hold in your thoughts, beliefs and subconscious. When you know, believe, accept and understand you are aspects of God (Love) and think, act and hold the vibration of that aspect of yourselves, you live in the kingdom of heaven.

"I accepted the persecution of the Romans and gave back love and forgiveness. I chose this form of death to prove the possibility of ascension and to prove there is life after death of the physical body."

# 6.

# Creation of This Universe

"The present religious scriptures are generally remnants or mistranslations of original Spiritual Teachings offered by God-enlightened Prophets, Masters, Swamis and Avatars thousands of years ago. Offered in ancient, now-dead languages, these teachings have been translated and mistranslated into other languages from century to century. They have been interpreted and misinterpreted by various scribes, cleric and theologians.

"Much of what Jehovah did was erroneously attributed to the Creator God. God has no personality. Jehovah and Yahweh, serving as Lords of Earth, were both beings with personality.

"Most of the stories in the Old Testament, which are erroneously attributed to the Creator God, are allegorical stories and not based on actual events. This is another reason that Humans need to become aware that the *Bible* is not the Word of God but full of personal ideas and mistranslations of Ancient Spiritual Teachings.

"The Creator God or Infinite Intelligence brought into expression 'Seven Spirits of Creation' who were referred to in Hebrew as 'Elohim'; they are sometimes in English referred to as 'The Builders of Form'. These Great Beings, using the Power and Attributes of the Creator, caused various energies to come forth and become dynamic. These Seven Spirits then manifested and materialized planets and star systems by causing a stepping-down, a slowing-down of vibratory frequency of the component atoms and electrons of Source energy.

"These Seven Spirits of Creation, the Elohim, presently express in your sector of this Omniverse. They include both male and female counterparts and are named: Apollo and Lumina; Arcturus and Victoria; Cyclopea and Virginia;Hercules and Amazonia; Heros and Amora; Peace and Aloha;

Purity and Astrea.

"What Humans call 'Nature', plants, animals and minerals, were created by the members of the Angelic Realm. There are seven Archangels who express in one of the seven Octaves or Rays, as do the Seven Spirits of Creation and also include both male and female counterparts.

"The seven Archangels that presently express in your sector of the Omniverse including male and female counterparts are named: Chamuel and Charity; Gabriel and Hope; Jophiel and Christine; Michael and Faith; Raphael and Mother Mary; Uriel and Aurora; Zadkiel and Amethyst.

"These Archangels serve to manifest various types of Life and Consciousness throughout this Universe. The Angelic level of creation that have brought forth and manifested the many types of life forms and different aspects of Nature upon the planets are called 'Devas'. Every life form on Earth has been created deliberately to create a balance of Nature. Each created form fulfills a certain purpose, need or function.

"Since the original manifestation of life forms and aspects of Nature, these seven Archangels have continued to manage and maintain their manifestations. Additionally, they have other responsibilities associated with protecting, teaching and guiding Human souls.

"These seven Archangels are involved in administering and controlling the seven Rays that the Source created and sent to Earth to assist Human evolution. They radiate these seven Rays to maintain, energize and nourish all forms and expressions of Life throughout this Universe, including Human, Elemental and Angelic.

"In addition to the seven Archangels, there are seven Ascended Masters who also have important responsibilities and great Spiritual Authority in the next level of the Brotherhood's Administrative Branch. Each of these Ascended Masters also express and serve in one of the seven Rays that represent Attributes of the Creator. These seven Ascended Masters, to complement the seven Archangels, govern, guide, supervise and teach these expressions of Life and Consciousness throughout your Universe which contains the twelve planets.

"This Universe is manifested, sustained and governed in a state of Divine Order, Harmony, Wisdom and Love in accord with the Creator's Will and Cosmic Law. The Spiritual Hierarchy is founded on Cosmic Wisdom and Divine Love and all Beings who are a part of it express as ONE, each expressing as an impersonal, selfless, inseparable Consciousness within the Creator's omnipresent Supreme Consciousness. All Spirit Beings, whether great Lords, Archangels, Masters or lower Orders of Angels each aid and serve the Hierarchy in a selfless manner. Each of the Beings also serve, in a selfless manner, the billions of Human souls and every aspect of planetary manifestation. They serve each in accord with their individual aptitudes and development of personal Attunement with the Creator's Attributes.

"Because of wise management from the Administrative Branch of this Great White Brotherhood (which is also referred to as the Spiritual Hierarchy) each of the twelve planets are maintained and governed in their orderly, precise orbit around the Sun. The members of the Administrative Branch and their Legions of Angels are not only responsible for bringing forth the Creator's Cosmic Power but also for maintaining the resulting energies. Their maintenance and application of the energies further includes a precise regulation for the orbits of many 'moons' around the planets. The required energies throughout each planet and all aspects of Nature are also sustained and governed in a continuous manner by these great Spiritual Beings and the many Angels, Devas and Nature Spirits that are involved in all of this Creation. Helios and Vesta are the Beings who control Earth's Sun.

"Though the Creator is omnipresent and fills all space throughout the Omnivers; however, in vast spaces between galaxies the Creator's Attributes are in a dormant, passive, non-expressive condition. As Pure Spirit and Consciousness occupying the limitless Omniverse, the Creator therefore needs Individualized Expressions of His Beingness in order to express His Attributes in specifically designated areas of the Omniverse. It is only from and through His Individualized Expressions of Life and Consciousness, His Image and Likeness in the form of Spirit Beings that the infinite Spirit and Consciousness of the Creator becomes fully expressive and creative.

"In your Universe it is therefore through the Great White Brotherhood that the seven-fold Creative Principle becomes activated and dynamic. These three Attributes of Wisdom, Love and Power are the primal trinity of the Creator that makes Creation possible. They are the foundational Principle of the Creator's Expression of Consciousness and Beingness.

"These Divine Attributes occur in varying degrees of expression among both Ascended Beings and unasceneded Humans only in accord with their Spiritual Attunement with the Creator and the purity of their consciousness.

"It is a definite requirement for every Human on Earth to return to his/her Divine Source. In order to accomplish this, one must mitigate and dissolve the accumulations of psychic illusions and delusions manifested during this and past embodiments. The Universal Law decrees that a

Human's negative karma, the sins, iniquities, omissions and commissions in opposition to Cosmic Law, must be less than the positive karma of 'good works' committed in compliance with the Law.

"To become an Ascended Being in the Great White Brotherhood of this Universe requires a purified consciousness. A consciousness must become Spiritualized as a God-enlightened Being to qualify to become a member of the Brotherhood as anything less would not be of any value in higher dimensions nor to the Brotherhood."

# 7.

# Earth Known as Dark Planet

"When I appeared on Earth as the one called Jesus, Humanity was totally ignorant of mechanical things and had no communication devices as you do today that could spread an understanding of what life is really all about. Humanity, then, was ignorant beyond description and Earth was well known as the dark planet of your solar system and your Universe. Little light existed and there was nothing of the mental understanding I could use to explain the working of God's twelve universes. That is why my examples and illustrations were all given simply to open the Human heart to God, to love, and the necessity for peace above all, which is the highest form of love.

"What could I say to a simple person about the workings of not one, but twelve universes? Or about twelve living planets and their life forms, each as a separate aspect of God's purpose in this solar system? And so I chose examples that would remain in the subconscious mind to be understood later. I chose the twelve disciples to represent the characteristics of God which Humanity must learn and balance.

"Humanity is limited now, but it once used this Earth as a mighty and glorious residence of immense beauty and love. Now see it as we see it, a place of darkness of the Spirit; a place of war and hatred. A place where Humanity has allowed its own fears to be expressed through military and governmental leaders who take fear, ignorance and evil to hurt your own living Mother Earth, and now Humans want to enter space where they will endanger other beings you cannot see but who also have life and eternal relationship in the great Oneness of creation.

"Humanity has entered into the scientific and technological arena without the proper love nature required before it is safe to explore such information. Your mechanization has outdistanced your soul. You are like an armed bomb ready to detonate by the next great negative thought.

"I hear you saying, 'I am not like that. I pay my taxes and go to work every day and tithe to the church and do good deeds. No, I am not responsible for the events of Earth or even of the government of this place where I live.' Truly do you deceive yourself. For if love and goodness prevailed, how then are your World events the way they are and why have you sent so much evil out into space? Know I am called upon by many other beings having residence in your Milky Way galaxy to tell you to cease this flagrant abuse of space. Space is protected by Galactic Law.

"I am not trying to paralyze you with guilt, for the limitation it brings emotionally does not assist you in making forward progress. But, I share these facts so that you may immediately implement an upgrading of your own behavior and share your concern in outspoken commitment. This is the time to be peace, but also the time to share it, for only by the sharing and multiplication of energy into a beautiful thought will the negative band of blackness in Mother Earth's emotional body be cleansed. Humans have soiled their dwelling place and must reverse that action. Earth, like you, has physical, emotional, mental and spiritual energy layers and is a massive reflection of your input to Her. Since you are a cell in Her body, be sure your influence is one of deep love, respect and appreciation for each unique and beautiful thing She nurtures upon Her body, upon Her surface.

"Whether you believe it or not, each planet is just as alive as you and is a great being of light and wisdom. You and your scientists must one day accept this truth, for it is your ignorance about life that allows the weaponry used beyond your borders where Earth's subtle bodies, non-physical essence, are violated. No sane people would annoy, aggravate, or injure any part of their mother, the land of their own existence, but this is what you do. Where will you be without Her for your substance? Beware you grasp these words, dear ones. Your lives depend on it. You must be caretakers of the Earth and the cooperative protectors of space; for this you were created.

"God created all. God is a force so powerful that your languages cannot describe it. The power of electricity and solar energy and radio and air flight and TV were always there, but you have only recently understood such principles. Realize how ignorant Humanity is and be still within you that you may learn further truth. It is through the transformation of your little consciousness into a greater reality and attunement with this great power that you grow and advance upon the Earth and within the solar system in which Mother Earth dwells.

"Within your earthly *Bible* is the statement 'Ye must become like little children to enter the kingdom of heaven.' That is true because children are open to learning, whereas most adult Earth dwellers are puffed up with self-importance based on the fact that your society says they have studied and are therefore knowledgeable; they are so called experts of it all. In fact, very few such experts, especially in the area of science, know much at all. Historians are even harder pressed to fit together pieces of a puzzle that clearly lacks a majority of the pieces. How, then, can such incomplete evidence, which ignores everything the Human eye cannot see, fit together pieces of a puzzle that clearly lacks a majority of pieces?

"The irony of it all is that rather than admit you do not know, the experts continue to parade their half-truths in the name of education and go unchallenged in their judgments. Give up your own petty understandings and ask your soul for the truth. Humans do not even understand where they came from or where they are headed.

"Your so-called scientists do not grasp your solar system's sun was breathed into its place about 218,000,000,000 years ago and it took nearly one million years before it was made habitable by the highly refined Light energies of the great beings who run this solar system. These energies, for which your language has no words, are as light furnaces in their creative nature and would dissolve you. Because of the higher vibrations and nature of their light, the Sun is their natural habitation. That is why I said you had to go through The Christ to know God, for God's power would unintentionally, but immediately, kill your body. The Christ I refer to is not a person, but a cosmic energy referred to as the Cosmic Christ Consciousness.

"In your Universe, the twelfth, there are twelve different solar systems with a total of 1,900,000 or nearly two million planets, busily using the energy of God. Each solar system has its own centralized power source (Solar Logos) and the individual twelve Rays of sound and light spectra not understood on Earth. The Earth has recently been gifted with 49 Rays of energy coming from the heart of God to increase the possibility of Humanity waking up to their own divinity. These are Rays of energy, each of which represent a particular aspect or facet of God, which Humans, in this solar system, are to use to develop Humanity into greater balance. Each Ray is administered by great beings of immense power and can be called forth by Humans once they accept that these Rays exist. Each Ray emits a color and each of these color streams of energy controls a certain aspect of creativity or influence. Earth is a unique planet, a Second Ray planet. The Second Ray is the focus for love and wisdom. It was for this that planet Earth was created, and it is only this which each soul living on Earth is to perfect.

"You are being infused with the Rays and the light of God as soul fuel or food and, unless your heart is open to love, you cannot bear the intensity and magnitude of their nature. Only Humans who are awake to their spirit will know what is happening and be able to utilize the love/wisdom Rays properly during the cleansing which will occur on Earth. Use your Freewill wisely.

"If you will use the Rays to strengthen God's purpose in you, the planet will rise into the heavenly realm by natural causes. But if Humanity insists on ignoring the Rays of love and wisdom or uses its Freewill in the wrong way, then Earth will have to be cleansed of the negative use of the Ray energies one way or another. The separation of loving and unloving souls is occurring. For as the power of the many spiritual energies assist at this time in bringing the love/wisdom Rays into perfection, all those souls who do not flow with this power will be unable to hear the change in their physical and subtle bodies.

"Knowledge of the whole spectrum of the 49 Rays of God has been gifted to Humanity. Seek this knowledge and use it to strengthen yourself and the Earth. If you cannot see the Rays and look only to what you can physically see, you miss what is now available to you. Be willing to acknowledge that you are limited and ask always that the higher forms of subtle life be made manifest to you, so Humans do not destroy Earth and space through this unfortunate ignorance and blindness.

"Who are you? You are a spiritual reality living in a physical body because it benefits your soul experience to do so. And in the vast mind of God, the Source of us all, a plan for many souls to expand the qualities of love and devotion was offered you. You accepted this opportunity for growth and expansion because that is the nature of God, for, by its division into many parts, it moves ever outward and achieves greater power and wisdom as it does. God and you are working together for the good of all, stretching farther and farther into distant regions of consciousness and love, which is an exciting and noble purpose.

"You chose to come to Earth because it provides you with the greatest challenge to grow and learn and to realize that your mind is the creator or architect or builder of whatever appears in the physical world. You came to learn and your soul chose this time and place to help you to develop your own personal soul evolution and the evolution of the Human family. You chose it, as you would select a course of study, knowing that the evolution of Earth Herself would be part of your, and Her, learning process.

"This was a deliberate choice not some accident of a fierce and cruel God. You have always existed and always will exist. The soul never chooses to remain idle; it chooses constant growth through experience. You ask, 'But why must I have a physical body?' Physical form is like a mirror for your soul, which intends to bring pure motive and intention into the personality. Spirit must penetrate the mental and emotional filters of each Human being in order to do this; any barriers caused by ignorance and misqualified information bring distortions which create pain. You have a body as a mirror of the soul so that you can see what false beliefs you hold and get rid of them. It is a 'mind over matter' suit, and its health and your life affairs are your constant progress report.

"You are Light and energy because that is what God is. You have temporarily come over the bridge from infinity into your present physical form. You contain all the truth you will ever need. And, because of your original identity as an aspect of God, you are capable of unlimited understanding. You must acknowledge this identity and then ask for its assistance. This is the key. This wiser you, massive in its abilities, can only keep in touch with you through your recognition and acknowledgment.

"The reason you need to hear the consequences of your own cause, or thoughts, from your mind is that the Universe in which you dwell is mental and is structured on twelve certain Laws, one of which is Cause and Effect. What is created in mind is the cause, and that which is experienced in the body is an effect. Unfortunately, many personalities do not recognize their responsibilities and constantly feel victimized by life, or by God, for what happens. While there are great beings of love and wisdom who direct the destiny of this planet from what you might call higher or inner dimensions, you are here to learn to use that mind power purely when you are again out of the body. This learning to use mind energy in only a positive way is critical if you are to grow and serve yourself, Humanity, the planet and God in reverence and devotion.

"What do you gain from asking for help if you do not follow the very prescriptions we give for understanding life's events and surrendering to lessons they contain? The answer is always the same and will always be the same: Love, Purity of thought and action. When the mind obeys the soul in these matters, it grows and advances into even higher levels of usefulness to itself and all of life.

"Understand that the things of this Earth which you call evil or negative, such as hunger, war or disease, are here to train you in the ways you view these and respond to them, for each soul may be on a different level of perfect mind usage and these experiences teach bold and often-times painful lessons which will never be forgotten. Famines and horrors serve Humanity, for they bring separated attitudes and beliefs into focus on identical issues, providing a common curriculum of teaching outline for love and peace. You are here to demonstrate self-mastery in the use of your mind and its thoughts or you would not be on the planet at this time. This is all opportunity which serves a higher purpose than your Human personality may realize.

"It may be difficult to see these events as valuable, as helping you to recognize balance from imbalance, love from fear. It is difficult to appreciate freedom unless you have been imprisoned or healthy unless you have been ill.

"You have a mind that can be trained to give up all personality judgments and achieve only positive responses to whatever Happiness in the World. Or, at least, the result will bring peace.

"You are not alone in this temporary existence unless you choose to be. There is never a time when the infusion of our power and love and guidance is denied you. But should there be an earthquake, for example, it may be impossible for us to get through your self-focused activities which are dearer to you than meditating and finding time to attune yourself to the helping frequency we would use. Often the inner teacher of each person is forgotten or never acknowledged as the key to freedom and joy.

"This living planet, which is often ignorantly referred to as a rock riding through space, is also part of God's plan for growth and service; for just as you have inner feelings and mental and spiritual aspects, so does She. Never doubt Earth has Her own destiny and never attack Her or you will attack the feminine nurturer within yourself. What you do to any other living thing must result in your own experience of it. If you do not understand the purpose and do not follow the rules, you will suffer pain. Yet, though your errors you will grow. Love is the balm for all wounds.

"Many of your holy books and written scriptures tell you there is an omniscient, omnipresent and ever-expanding force, source of energy which is called by many names in many languages. 'God' will do. Most of these teachings say that this God constantly moves and grows, gaining further power with the development of each being that is a smaller part of the whole.

"Space contains a myriad of life forms mostly unknown to you in your extremely limited definition of life. Be cautious how you treat space and move ever so slowly as if you were in a darkened room filled with precious breakable objects which you must not injure. Part of space contains the extended life energy fields of your own Mother Earth and She suffers from your spaceships and weaponry as it blasts through Her invisible energy fields. Sound, heat, light and color energy Rays are everywhere present, moving unrestrictedly from lighter, higher energy to denser forms. As you learn about these energies, you can earn your place among those who will respect and honor them and call upon them to assist in many situations.

"The vital impression I wish to impart here is, Earth is a very small planet physically and is part of a solar system family from whom all are fed by the Sun's life energy. The Sun and these higher level Beings feed and fuel the life force of your solar system, Earth and yourself without ceasing. They deserve recognition. Your two greatest difficulties are Freewill and doubt. Your lack of appreciation for the gift of life and sustaining support to Earth must be corrected. It is wise to be reverent.

"Once the Earth glowed with an etheric light of such beauty she was known as the jewel of this quadrant of the Universe. This was before Humans were established on Earth. Know the governmental body, the Milky Way galaxy, is the homeland of many great Beings, Luminaries, energies and the vibrations who have their residence there and who have profound spiritual effect upon the Earth.

"It is important to remember some souls chose to come to Earth in a mass immigration plan, in a spirit body, to begin this newly made planet about eight million years ago. The intention was to make a wonderful learning place within this solar system and this galaxy, a place where love and wisdom would reach a high plane of expression. So you are not here by accident nor were you always in this dense form which now encases your soul in physical flesh.

"Most religions speak of a separation or fall in Humanity's past, so there is much I could share about this sinking of consciousness into its present pitiable condition. To avoid guilt, however, is my goal, for it freezes your ability to change and move forward. Therefore, let me just say that what is gone is gone. Whether you are a visitor from some other starseed or merely an unlearned or lightless soul, you are needed here now. Humankind's future depends upon your commitment to have peace and nothing but peace.

"Many of the civilizations in this galaxy were not given the capacity for heart love and could use an example to emulate for they are focused entirely on the intellectual aspect of life. You of Earth, who were intended to become a pattern which extends love to these mental beings, have much to learn from these other ones but also much to teach of the feeling nature of mortality. You can teach how to love God totally while sealed in a Human body. You could be described as energy living in matter, remembering itself as that greater love identity. This was the plan undertaken nearly eight million years ago here by the spiritual and etheric realms from which some of you emerged and are a part.

"Some souls, such as you, volunteered to be here until the plan was achieved and Earth was in concert with the other planets in both the solar system and the galaxy as that place where demonstration of love of God and all life forms could be witnessed and experienced. Let each person on the Earth acknowledge that behavior is the test of knowing. Imagine if you were from another branch of God's creation: Would you wish to meet the present day earthlings as your model of peace? Your present assaults on your own Earth's energy fields, and upon those brothers and sisters in space, have made you suspect indeed. If the situation were reversed and you were the technically superior, might you not also watch Earth with suspicion, as it spews forth killer satellites and threatens other life forms with nuclear blasts and plans to deliver even greater destructive weaponry? In my position as World Teacher, I am making this attempt to change the abysmal reputation Earth has gained.

"There is a legion of volunteers ready to help Earth's rebirth and Humanity's awakening. This legion will be used by those of us in the spiritual realms in case Earth's experiment goes astray due to nuclear disaster or by a response from the Earth Herself to eliminate Humanity's accumulated violence and negative emotions. Doubt is a great enemy and the most deleterious of attitudes to hold. It is only in your willingness to trust the unseen that you grow. Doubt has retarded many Human souls. It leaves no room for hope, no access to peace. Doubt is the inner enemy of Humanity and is created in the mind.

"Keep your faith high, and realize in a few years the spiritual cleansing will remove those souls who will not honor God or hear the inner voice of God. The meaning of faith, which is to trust the Creator, is to implement the Divine Plan in the best possible way. Faith requires you to follow your inner teacher, your inner knowing, that spark of God given to you when your individual soul was created eons ago. Meditate daily and join with others to pray for healing the planet and all those upon it. Have faith and be strengthened by your own inner guidance which is the gift to all who ask and demonstrate their sincerity by meditation. Simply say, "Take my doubt Father/Mother God. I am willing to let my heart and soul be filled with only love and faith. "

# 8.

# Jesus Speaks Today On Historical Records of Earth

"To understand my appearance on the Earth nearly 2,000 years ago you need a framework and a context in which to hold the information, or it makes little sense to the intelligent mind, the seeking heart. But I warn you the truth will probably startle you because the historical records of this planet have been so decimated over the eons of time that you hardly know any truth about its geology, its geography, its people or their activities. Therefore, you do not understand the truth.

"Regrettably your text books in the schools have done little to further the truth because only a modicum is provable by the actual evidence you now perceive. Land and cultures have come and gone and many lie under miles of ocean water or mountain debris beyond your direct knowledge. Only with recent photographic techniques used in space, looking back at Earth, do your geologists begin to see the actual physical evidence beneath the Earth's surface.

"I choose to share an abbreviated history of Earth with you so you can begin to grasp the enormity of your present situation and understand the reasons why a World Teacher like me came to Earth 2,000 years ago to bring this 250,000 year phase of Humanity's spiritual evolution to conclusion.

"Let your intuition, your knowingness and connection to your soul confirm what I say. This is the ending of an era, the ending of an Age, the ending of my leadership over the Earth in the way your scriptures reported me as Jesus of Nazareth. I have grown and expanded, as have many of you. My essence is now with the Cosmic Christ Consciousness even as I serve as World Teacher with part of my energy guiding planet Earth and Humanity.

"Life in its spiritual dimension has existed about eight million years above Earth's surface in the etheric realm and life before Earth is trillions of years old. Earth is part of the 12th Universe, and the other eleven took many eons to develop under the Creator's original design. The 12th Universe is younger but has greater variety than the others.

"There are literally millions of planets in some of these universes. Many of them have living things, not only in plant, bird, animal and mineral life, but creations of what you call spiritual bodies, as well as some physical forms like your own and others which you cannot even imagine. You are not alone in this Universe, although many of your space brothers and sisters are different in size, build, light density, and mental capacity. There are many life forms because our Father/Mother God has been experimenting over a million years to learn what types of life are most effective and what is most pleasing as a creation. The Source created all of these beings.

"These twelve universes each have a different purpose and a different type of experimentation to suit the Creator's plans. There are no words in your written language to explain God, the universes, the heavens and dimensions. We use light packets and pictures and sound instead of verbal communication. God or the Source, the Creator of all that is, is beyond physical description. God has a form of immense size and of a blinding glow beyond description. God has an enduring and passionate love for everything of its creation. You are the children of a great being who loves you.

"One day all of Humanity who have chosen to return to God will lose the density of the physical body and become a form of light containing both male and female principles in balanced proportions. Heaven is not an idle place. Its many activities require loving and devoted family members to work harmoniously in the organization and maintenance of God's Creations. In your *Bible* it is mentioned I said, 'In my father's house there are many mansions.' This is a 'miss translation' of 'in my father's house there are many dimensions.'

"I will describe the twelve universes which our Father/Mother God created, including Earth's position therein. In your local Universes there are twelve parts, or solar systems, and Earth's position is the smallest of the dozen solar systems in your Universe. These other created universes preceded yours. If you accept this, you will better understand the present situation in which Earth finds Herself.

"My own Universe was created first and has one beautiful solar system with only two planets produced by the Creator in an act of intense love and imagination. While I was on Earth, a part of my energies remained in my Universe.

"There are additional universes which were experiments following the first one. There is a second Universe in which the Creator made all beings of female nature, the love of nurturing side of God, and the third Universe which has only male attributes or the will, power and active aspects of God. Both of these universes are of such a high vibration you could not see them with the Human eye, just as most Earth dwellers cannot see me and the Angelic hosts.

"In these separate universes, both the males and females could independently reproduce offspring with the breath, even as God ordained it. They needed no sexual counterpart. This is a spiritual dimension strange to your own body limitations. Those of you who have difficulty with the so-called 'virgin birth' may now see it in a new light.

"The 4th Universe was created following the experience in which male and female principles were separated from each other. They were recombined in the 4th Universe since love and power should be together and not kept apart. This is a soul essence and quality I speak about, not your dense physical flesh which came eons later after the other Universes were completed.

"In the 5th Universe the power of mind thought, which is different from intellect, was developed. This entire Universe kept one primary, unified thought, or intention, to love God, paramount, even though the souls were separated. By your standards this was miraculous. In Humans you need a love purpose to direct energy into thought or you will misuse it. A thought is energy moving its intention into reality. Thoughts are alive. Mind requires a heart's love for wholeness. Intellect is only 50% of thought. When intellect and intuition, or God's knowingness are combine, there is perfect balance. In the 5th Universe the inhabitants did so well they were allowed to return to the Creator en masse and it is now an unpopulated area in what you call space. Never did an entire Universe grasp the love principle and practice it so perfectly.

"The 6th Universe is a place where the miniaturization of life forms was stressed so the inhabitants are tiny in size, the planets are smaller than most, and the beings love God devotedly as their acts of producing beautiful natural things, such as flowers, prove. The descendents of these tiny creations living on your Earth's etheric plane are often called nature spirits by those with the clairvoyant power to see them. They are dedicated to bring flower and plant life to its highest form.

"In the 7th Universe of eight million planets, one million are inhabited, the male and female beings were focused solely in the area of intellectual expertise focused. They focused primarily on mathematical science. There was no love side to their nature for one another or for the Creator. Here it was learned intellect in male or female without the balance of heart love is not desirable. This 7th Universe is still functioning. Science is a God-made thing not the work of mere mortals who claim it as theirs. A true scientist can only discover Universal Law or principle to fulfill life's function and use it for the good of all. In fact, every scientist is obligated to seek reverently for God's principles, with the intention of applying them only for the common good.

"In the 8th Universe of four million planets, our Creator caused a million to be inhabited and did a variety of experiments to understand the effects of the Rays upon matter. Here some beings were given almost X-Ray vision, others were imbued with the Rays of heat, magnetism and electricity and were able to oscillate and levitate. Some of the experiments involved temperature changes and effects from excessive dark and light exposure. These creations underwent the experiments for the good of the life forms which would follow them. In the Omniverse all of God's creations have their plans and purposes. Each builds upon the prior gifts of the ones before it. Your position in the 12th and last Universe, while God's purpose is to bring you home, you have the aspects of all this learning at your disposal if only you seek and synthesize it.

"The 9th Universe, with only about 900 inhabited planets, was a spacious and unusual experiment. These people were focused on their spiritual natures and the love of God so constantly and consistently this area is now empty of them. Merely a perfumed hush of peace remains in the ethers from their gentle natures. Because of their deep devotion to our Creator they all had the gifts of clairvoyance, clairaudience and mediumship. Some went home to God and some were reborn into your 12th Universe to help others to develop their spiritual gifts.

'Unlike their predecessors of the 9th Universe, the, the 10th Universe creations are attentive only to the matters of theology or the study of comparative religions throughout the many universes. With only 10% of some 900 planets inhabited they spent their time thinking and learning. In their theological colleges they would study these different teachings, in an intellectual way, seeking to know God only with their mind. Knowing a Human's mental definition of the Creator and experiencing that love in the heart are two very different things. It was my purpose here 2000 years ago to bring the experience and teachings of love back to Earth again, as others had done before and since.

"The 11th Universe of Mechanism could not have existed save for the focus on engineering. However, of the men and women from these million-and-a-half planets, all but those on two planes were decimated by war. The great inventiveness of thought without love's influence, their designs led to military uses. Although the warfare was carried out primarily by the machines they had invented, at least 860 of God's planets were decimated by the violence.

"They feared God, but they held no heart love to soften their inventive genius. The life forms chose machinery over God, and their inventions became their masters. They eventually could not regain control over their creations, what their thoughts created eventually destroyed them.

"You may be recognizing these same kind of effects happening in your own 12th Universe today. Those of you who inhabit the planet Earth, along with about 500 other 12th Universe planetary forms, are now caught up in that possible destructive aspect of engineering mechanization. Most other planets in the 12th Universe are superior to Earth in technology but so far Humans refuse to acknowledge this fact along with the Interdimensional presence of other life forms.

"Since you have the mixture in this 12th Universe of all the other eleven in varying amounts and combinations, your 12th Universe is a potpourri. It is all here from those trillions of years of learning and growth that have already transpired before.

"Your 12th Universe is the largest of all that has preceded you. It has the greatest variety of learning possibilities to use, and the most tremendous opportunity to learn from past mistakes and past glories. All strengths and weaknesses of these past experiences are available to you. You must choose wisely in your Universe and competently amalgamate or synthesize the best of it all, denying the ill-fated mechanization which manifested so widely and destructively in the 11th Universe. Humanity must focus more clearly on love than ever before if you wish to return to God purified of violence. Return is scheduled soon for many, but only the loving ones can proceed.

"I wish to speak about your own solar system which is in the 12thUniverse, and about your so-called space programs. You might ask your scientists who send astronauts and instruments looking for other life to expand their own consciousness and stop wasting so much time and money looking for things in the Third Dimensional World. Most life on the other planets operates in the etheric levels of the Fourth dimension and beyond. That which does not would not wish your warlike attitudes to locate them anyway. Your three dimensional eyes and instruments are blind to these other dimensions. So do not be surprised you do not find life, as you know it, on the planets in your own solar system. "Humans currently suffer from spiritual amnesia. When Human consciousness advances into Fourth dimensional realities you will see other life forms.

"I have admonished you as a species not to take violence or weaponry of any kind into space but it is permitted to pursue totally peaceful research projects of a truly reverent or scientific nature. When you enter space, unless your crew is clairvoyant do not expect to see other life. Earth Humans are nearly the lowest forms of consciousness in the known solar system at this time, which is why the Earth is being bombarded with the high frequency of light vibrations in hope of awakening a sleeping race.

"All of heaven in its multidimensional reality is presently involved in an enormous expenditure of energy that you are incapable of grasping and apparently even appreciating. We will continue to follow God's decree to assist all who will agree to awaken. These additional energies of love and power that are coming to you represent one of the greatest commitments that millions of us beyond your sight are giving. They are the same type of consciousness acceleration that your so-call Renaissance times in Europe and the other golden Ages of wisdom in the Orient and elsewhere represent, only multiplied by a much higher factor.

"The many others who wait to awaken until later in this century probably cannot do so without pain and suffering. The longer the personality resists its awakening, the more profound the experience the soul must bring to ignite awareness. For some people this may be very intense.

"Your soul, bj, will put your personality to the test of self-mastery for it was this achievement you desired."

# 9.

# Earthbound History Is Over Universal History Has Begun

The purpose of the current crisis is to awaken and activate within us new talents and capacities. It is time for the marriage between our faith and knowledge. It is time for us to co-operate consciously with the Creator of all Universes. The ultimate reality is not matter, but patterned intentional energy, GOD.

Our job is to work now with Creation to achieve the next level of consciousness, freedom and order in this World and the Universe beyond. There is a Designing Intelligence in the Universe. We are the creations of that Intelligence. We are designed to be self-evolving and to be conscious co-creators. In order to act out the next chapter in the history of the World and Universe we must become conscious co-creators with the Intelligence of GOD. We are an infinitesimal part of an infinite Universe. We are one body born into this Universe seeking greater awareness of our Creative Intention. We are capable, even in our infancy, of resonating with that Infinity to an ever more precise degree. We can accomplish this by conscious integration of our intention with the Will of GOD. Our rational thought processes often come between us and our immediate sensing of God's will. Our consciousness is both infinite and eternal. We are the bridge between the Creator and matter. It is critical that we remember our origins and purpose. We must consciously rejoin the Cosmic Family.

You are not the form you animate, but the force of animation itself.

We have a mission to trace the steps we have taken to become awake and to share those steps with others. We are to practice and thereby teach by example "response-ability," the ability to respond to our souls.

For the next level of evolution to take place dominion over nature must become co-creation with nature. Individual creativity must become synergistic co-operation. The next quantum leap must be from self-centered to co-creative, universal consciousness.

Our progress as a species has been stymied by our lack of vision of what the power of the Sun, the power of the World, the power of God is for. The true purpose of Human genius is the creation of Universal Life.

We are called to focus upon the Intelligence manifested in the exquisite organization and design of every entity from sub-atomic particles to the Human brain. Recognize in yourself the essence of that Intelligence. View yourself as a personal participant in the evolution of the Universe—a co-creative member of the on-going creation.

Do not frustrate the "grace of GOD" the "will of GOD" by ignoring the truth of who you really are. Relax your figuring-it-out mind, to allow your deeper knowing to speak. You are an agent of the "Creative Intention: experimenting for GOD. There is a design, but it is flexible. Believe for an instant that the Universe is alive and attracted to you as you are attracted to it.

Jesus was a version of the future Human, an evolutionary template. The capacities to do as He did are activated in us only through agreement and expectation.

When we discover our life purpose we are changed. We enter a new life cycle. We are no longer aging, and dying, we are growing and evolving. We are here to create in the landscape of time and matter.

Perfection is not ever making a mistake;, perfection is never consciouslymaking a mistake.

You are not your body. You are not your thoughts. You are not what you feel, not your roles or your experience. You are the Spirit of Life itself dancing in clay delighting in the glorious opportunity of incarnation exploring the realms of matter, blessing the Earth and all therein.

There is a new vibrational pattern descending upon the Earth through the Sun flares packets of information are exploding in our atmosphere. This information comes in living information units called the Language of Light. They convey organic information of concise, yet comprehensive, informational content. It is important for us to focus our attention on inner vibrational frequencies. This is information that comes to us from the Source of our being. The information is transmitted neurobiologically. The purpose of the information is to teach us of our own nature and purpose upon the Earth, to teach us to bridge the gap between our present condition and our true nature. We are being offered an opportunity to tune in to these new frequencies and find our lives growing more wondrous every day. Agree to unlock your own latent informational input systems. We were designed to be the central control mechanism of this planet.

Those who tune in to fear will find things in their lives falling apart. Two Worlds of consciousness are forming even more distinctly; the World of Love and Life and the World of fear and death. The vibrations on Earth will continue to increase. It will be far better for us to break the patterns in our life that are not in harmony now, on our own, than to wait until the increasing vibrational intensity that is enveloping the Earth's atmosphere breaks them for us. We can continue to trust in fear and reason or we can trust GOD implicitly and the truth of GOD'S Divine Design will be revealed in every situation. Specific information for each situation is being supplied to us constantly by the Source of Infinite Knowledge. We have all the pertinent information in the Universe available to us simply for the asking.

We have been imprisoned in our concepts of what's possible.

The next stage of Human and Earth evolution involves our extraterrestrial friends over lighting various animal species on the Earth. Since Humans are still too warlike for our ET friends to show up to help us looking like they normally do they have chosen, with our permission, the Sirians are now in addition to being here for centuries in the form of dolphins and whales and the giant squid they are over lighting many of the large dog forms, such as the Labrador retrievers, chows, Afghan hounds, Mastives, Rottweiler's, etc.

At the time the book and movie the Horse Whisperer came out the beings from Andromeda and Arcturus began to over light the equestrian population. Since then many of the other ET's are over lighting other animal forms, especially the ones with big eyes. We have seen a great increase in tolerance between various animal species that are not usually tolerant of each other. Weekly more and more of the evidential photos show up on the Internet. More and more animal/Human communication is sought and accomplished.

We now have two species of Humans cohabitating on Earth the Homo sapiens and the new Human version the Homo universalis. All beings born since 1985 are members of the new species. They have an etheric four quadrant brain and an etheric twelve strand helix of their DNA.

The next stage of evolution involves the anchoring of enormous Cities of Light over different areas of the planet. This process has begun.

We are designed to become Planetary Beings and then Universal Beings. GOD'S definition of us in form is much greater than any of us could possibly imagine for ourselves. We are being given the opportunity to embrace this true definition of ourselves as aspects of GOD operating in Human form. Our form is an identity a specific cell in a specific organ of a larger being --our Oversoul. We oscillate back and forth between our pre-manifest state and our species role form. To remain unconscious of our true identity with the Creator cuts off the flow of Light-giving information to the part of us that exists in form. Our identity with God is the reality from which all Life springs.

We are the bridge between Spirit and matter, between Creator and Creation, between Life and the forms through which Life flows.

We have a responsibility to adjust our vibrational patterns to more thoroughly accommodate the flow of Spirit through us.

Everything we need exists in this present moment, and this moment is all that exists. It is important that we recognize the creative power of our thoughts, a power far beyond our present knowledge. We were born to share GOD'S creative power. Through us GOD is revealed in material form.

# 10.

# Jesus Speaks on Religious Guidelines

"I came 2000 years ago to guide Humanity into this present opportunity for spiritual ascension as have many other great teachers of the past. The purpose of religion should be to connect Humans to God through their Human personalities and direct communication with their souls. Therefore, every organized institution held in my name is herewith ordered to examine its rituals and to change them if they do not include a time of quiet meditation. The membership should be allowed and encouraged to sit quietly for twenty minutes as part of the service, to hear what God would say to each one. A message may be given and the use of music is uplifting, but the critical part of the time should be spent in quietude with the soul.

"You still have the same commandments to love and not kill or harm. You live in a zone of temptation and negativity. This Third Dimensional zone requires you to cross the veil between what you see with your physical sense and what you know exists from your own soul level. For this, a bridge is necessary. Meditation, prayer and contemplation form that bridge. Churches must implement and encourage this practice. Otherwise, many who seek to build the bridge to God in meditation will be forced to go outside the present church organizations.

"As your World Teacher and as representative of the love/wisdom Ray for planet Earth, I recommend daily prayer and meditation to remind you of your connection to God. I came to demonstrate Humanity's immortal soul nature. That which you call death is only an upgrading of your physical body into a form of glowing light that is eternal and ongoing. By my resurrection you were shown the model or pattern you yourself acquire at the time you presume you die. You came to die. However, and this is critical, what you think and the way you act do have an effect on both your Earth life and your after Earth live.

"Since soul essence lives forever, your first requirement as a Human being is belief in God, belief in the nature of your soul and your certainty of a beforelife and an afterlife. It matters not which World religion you follow if it takes you to God with clarity and certainty that death is not the end. Let us have unity about our love for God within the diversity of the various groups and not separate ourselves as superior or as more beloved than others. Do not be self-righteous! It is an easy trap.

"The greatest gift any religion can give its members and participants are to place them in touch with their own inner teacher so their awareness of death, as a transition process, becomes certain. The way religions teach about this transition from matter back to energy and the rituals they have about it vary greatly, but the idea or theme should be the same. There is life after physical death.

"God loves all Human beings and does not judge them. You have judged yourselves, and, therefore. others; I recommend you relinquish judgment and accept love and forgiveness for everything real or imagined that has been done by you and others. The focus of my appearance was to bring love and institute forgiveness, to bring simplicity.

"I am disappointed so-called Christian religions held in my name are filled with pomp and grandeur that distinguishes the priest and ministers as the only ones who know God and from the congregation as those who do not or cannot personally know God. This subservience is erroneous as a pattern for love. Love accepts and is in partnership with all others. Temporary assistance may be given, but no one person is more entitled to or worthy of God's love than any other person. These theological differences are a Human limitation and prevent upward spiritual progress.

"I came to Earth 2000 years ago and said to Humanity 'For you are the light of the World.' I did not expect churches with glorious robes and artifacts of gold to be established in my name. I did not expect people to seize power in the name of God and to perpetrate their individual need for glorification through the use of my name. I did not expect Jew and Gentile to be separated or Christians pitted against followers of Buddha, Krishna or Mohammed. No, I did not. But look what has happened.

"This planet's formula for spiritual growth has been undermined by those evil, egotistical personalities whose need for power has overcome them and short-circuited the opportunity for Humanity's spiritual return to God. Still the plan will unfold as these structures and rigidities of spiritual limitation are released or destroyed.

"I ask every soul to consider whether its minister, priest, rabbi, guru or teacher is in direct connection with God and is intentionally bringing each of its charges into direct guidance from God. If religion, or group, in which you practice your belief and love of God is not bringing to you the opportunity for full spiritual development and soul growth through direct revelation and inner knowing, then you should leave that group and find another that is focused on direct soul communication.

"You need not cling to ritualistic practices, but may begin your own connections to God directly through your soul. No longer should financial support be given to those organizations that do not bring you a personal connection and experience of God. If your churches and your temples do not bring you into the fruition of your growth, then they do not serve you and must be abandoned now.

"The truth is all sons and daughters of all colors, religions and nations are welcomed in God's family if they choose it. But each individual soul has a unique path which gives different opportunities and expanding levels of growth both on Earth and in the heavenly realms beyond. Because your depth of love and service create the type of assignment or activity here and in the many dimensions of the Universe you have been advised to practice love and to give caring to others. For it is upon this record that you receive, by magnetic attraction, the next experience. Spiritual progression has always been a part of God's plan for Humanity's evolution, because there is much to learn and demonstrate before you are fully healed of negativity and ready for the potential opportunity that awaits.

"Surely you cannot imagine Earth life is all there is. That would be amusing. Open your minds if you've ever held such a thought. You are not ignorant peasants of yesteryear any longer. Your technology has brought you to the brink of a so-called Space Age. God is there, everywhere present. Do not doubt. Your religious teachings must include this expanding awareness of life beyond your own tiny planet.

"Religion must inspire Humanity to know more and use what it learns with love. Always love. This is the never ending commandment to every religion. Love is the actual energy of substance of which the Universe is made and held in place. Without it we would all perish. It is not some un-important ingredient of life without priority. Love is your primary obliga-tion on this planet, and if you deny yourself love, you will become stunted, probably ill. It is always your choice, by God's gift of Freewill.

"Those of us in the heavenly realms, which even now beckon you onward, work as a team to develop Humanity's abilities and attitudes. No one who wishes to grow will be overlooked. Your every desire to know and serve God will bring you higher and higher in the universal scheme of things. You will understand my mission, and your own, more fully. For now just accept this is so and that death is merely the end of a single drama with many soul activities remaining. This tapestry of becoming a worthy companion to God, and of divesting your personality of its limitations, should be the true teaching of any belief system, philosophy or church. Without imagination, love and joy something is missing in spiritual teachings.

"I promise you any church which deifies me instead of acknowledging God is behaving erroneously and should stop immediately. You pray and meditate in God's house; however, God can be experienced anywhere.

"Sit by a stream, if you can find an unpolluted one, listen to birds singing, and examine a tiny flower for its exquisite expression of symmetry and color. Amidst this variety, feel the presence of God's unending love for you. Allow your heart to expand and reach out to the animal life, things of the sea and water. God's original design called for all life forms on the planet to be interdependent and symbiotic. There should be cooperative, mutually beneficial relationships between Humanity and the animal, plant and mineral kingdoms.

"All of Humanity must assume responsibility as caretakers of the Earth. This, as in all things, is a Freewill decision bearing cause and effect in every individual's life. Higher levels of meditation and mental telepathy with us in Spirit are difficult to reach by those without compassion. Alcohol and drugs can destroy the spiritual fabric of your mind and emotions as well as bring misfortune to the body. Do not risk this potentially disastrous effect of drinking and drugs. The Aquarian Age will require disciplined minds and clear emotions and attitudes of non-violence. Use nothing in your body which puts you out of control of your peaceful behavior. Use nothing foreign as a substitute for a peaceful mind and loving heart.

"The churches of the World have much to do, and it is not just going to Sunday meeting to praise Jesus, I assure you. Let your coming together in love serve God, serve Humanity and serve peace. Let us devote our time to peace above all things for the planet is in a serious and threatened condition. It is endangered. Do all you can to speak peace and model peace. Teach its ways by your own behavior. This is the purpose of any religion, to strengthen the soul's practice of love and peace. So be peaceful with one another, in or out of church, and serve those in need. As you learn on Earth to practice the teachings of our Creator, you will earn the higher opportunity that awaits you at the time you call death.

"The purpose of any church, ashram, temple, cathedral or place of prayer and meditation is to teach the love of God above all things. It is not to deify one World Teacher or any combination of them. It is to appreciate and understand their teachings so much that you practice and live them. Your prostrations, which are not followed with everyday applications, are useless.

"Love for me is shown by your behavior, not by grandiose buildings and expansive organizations. These often detract from love's true mission. Love any and all World Teachers by the actions of your daily life. Conduct your business as if a World Teacher were in your store or conference room. Love and cooperation are vital everywhere. Many a soul has lost its way in the greed of commerce. My message to those in religious occupations is that it is your responsibility to teach everyone they have an inner teacher, the Holy Spirit, the soul knows its life purpose and blueprint designed by God.

"Theology is usually useless and argument over scripture is wasted energy. Take the theme of loving and live it. When you give the love of your hearts to those who wish to know God more intimately, you will be fulfilling your purpose. It is required you expand your present limitations in thinking about me and our Creator if you are to achieve self-mastery.

"If you cleave only to the exact word of a holy book which was released as a guide for past time rather than practicing the basic concepts expressed therein you will not be growing in the way God wishes. Your interpretation of all holy books must be expanded to recognize the higher vibrations now being transmitted to the planet Earth. Some insist the *Bible* is the final work or that the Koran is absolute truth and there will be no more prophets. To these ideas I say a resounding 'NO.' Life is growth and, therefore, change is inevitable. This New Age is the Age of transition when you must take the prior teachings to a higher level of understanding based on present World knowledge.

"If your prior training resists furiously, hear me through. It will be your key to expanding your growth in the coming years. Keep the simple truth of yesteryear, but allow it to flow upward as you further exemplify it into a higher interpretation of experience.

"The One God has sent many teachers to Earth over eons of time, leaving on the planet many World religions which seem today to separate Humankind into various camps and groups. Separation was never the

Creator's intention. The teachers were to pull Human forgetfulness back into true knowing of oneness, not to create divisions and further boxes.

"Your challenge today is to see the universal message that runs through all the World religions and to amalgamate the theme 'Oneness,' to go beyond your present divisions and separations. That is why I came, to combine all Humans into Oneness, but Humanity failed to understand me. There has never been any one code of teaching which will not need to be updated, aside from its one basic message of peace, love and forgiveness.

"God is assisting Humankind's return home in an evolving progress one step at a time, like a circling spiral ever moving upward to levels of greater awareness and unity, bliss and joy. As you become wiser in each higher understanding of basic truth which appears and reappears in different guises, your soul becomes more purified and able to demonstrate by its behavior that it has truly learned that one truth.

"Change is difficult for the Human personality; however, it will balk at having to rearrange the information drummed into it through habit and misqualified data. How long ago was it, Dear Ones, that Human beings believed the World was flat? Or that the Solar System revolved around the Earth instead of the Earth around the Sun? You could not fly until recently, but the knowledge of how to do it has always been there. Your return to God takes steps. The plan is sure and, like a river, offers continuous flow of deepening ideas and spiritual comprehension for those who will choose to know.

"There can be only one basic truth, brought to you over and over again in higher sequence of understanding and application. With each new flow of God's energy you can go to an increased level of knowing who God really is and how relevant you are to God's plan. You grow by incorporating new applications of God's energy. I ask you to accept this new level of understanding which I now bring to assist Humanity's accelerated return to the Fourth dimension, one step nearer God. For there are more and more rungs on the ladder than you have ascended.

"If you cling to every phrase of the Bible and argue its interpretation, you miss the point of God's message. Simply accept its basic tenet that you have a Creator, a powerful force who has a plan for your return home in love and forgiveness. Accept this promise. Live it. Enjoy the full measure of its healing. Following this plan is your function here.

"Since my coming to Earth 2,000 years ago, Humans have learned to take a gigantic scientific step. Now Humans must match it with the spiritual growth it requires. Your scientists must connect to their inner teachers of

God to see their relationship from a new vantage point or else they will harm the planet and leak misery into the Universes beyond. Humans are still children in their demonstration of love and peacefulness, but some have become scientific monsters without conscience or respect for God's firmament or Human life. This discrepancy in some Humans' behavior must stop.

"The limited scientific background of Humans on Earth 2,000 years ago could not grasp what your mind can grasp now. When I used the term, 'in my father's house are many mansions,' Humans were not capable of understanding I meant many dimensions of existence. Humans are presently behaving as ignorant children playing with such horrible tools of destruction as biological and physical weapons. Angels lament and other life forms watch from their space craft with justified horror and concern. Your governments cannot continue to hide the truth of these other civilizations out of fear.

"I now come to speak with you again. Humanity is off course and drifting further and further away from God's plan for Earth and Humanity. Humanity must give up negative thoughts and actions, war and violent thoughts. Since your group endeavor cannot progress until Humanity's emotions are cleansed, all Humans must release false beliefs and psychological limitations.

"I came to teach you love. The other dimensional civilizations cannot abide the evilness and sickness your technologists plan to bring into outer space. There is a ban, a quarantine on Earth, until all people, of their own Freewill, return to the Creator. Your surrender is not to me, but to your souls as they are powerful, loving and awesome. You must surrender your little will in order to follow the greater knowing.

"Humans are currently in three dimensional physical bodies with soul consciousness at the Fourth level. My role as World Teacher was, and is, to prepare you for the fourth dimensional level of soul love, or higher responsibility as energy living in matter. Your preparation time is over. Stand ready to affirm or deny your spiritual ascension, no matter your earthly path. I am with you now in thought to encourage your efforts of self-discovery and expansion.

"You are not alone in this huge Universe. Many life forms of varying sizes and shapes abound. Though you are only one blink in the vastness of eternity, you are important in the Creator's mind. Prepare yourself for this cosmic initiation by agreeing to turn within and take hold of the lifeline which will be provided through meditation, prayer and contemplation.

Meditation is the tool for the Aquarian Age. Every soul has the opportunity for the inner truth and the inner certainty.

"These new teachings are not based only upon past religious documents; I do not say this to you lightly, for the past religious teachings have been useful. They have been a necessary part of a Divine Plan of recollection and remembrance to bring you back to the heart of God, to bring you back to the eternal flow of God's mind and the Oneness of all living things. Nonetheless, I say to you today that in their place will come the inner teacher within each soul, which will again be reunited with the Creator and will become the funnel and the channel of love to bring you home again.

"The church structures as you know them are suspect. God's church is the same church I spoke of 2,000 years ago in Jerusalem and what every true teacher has spoken to you about every time period before and since. God's qualities are within you. Be still and listen to their message.

"As each soul awakens and returns to God through its daily meditation and through its weekly experience of sharing in groups in a prayerful way, the planet can yet be healed and a resurrection of Humankind achieved. Those who can expand their belief will advance under my tutelage but not if they worship me as a dead thing of the past, as the Godlike figure your organized churches have made me. Remember I still live and I have grown.

"My love is the Creator's love. My service is an expression of that. Let yours be the same. You are already the Christ consciousness, dear ones; you've simply forgotten. Acknowledge God. Cleanse your negative emotions and follow the guidance to an ongoing higher understanding.

"We are moving from an Age of Structure and form into the Golden Age of Aquarius, the Age of Inner Knowing. It is the gift of God to all beings. You can find your own inner soul connection and assist everyone else to do the same. You can be connected directly into the knowing of God's mind through your soul. I leave you today with this thought and my love.

# 11.

# Jesus Suggests Guidelines For Science and The Rays

"To live a life of appreciation for God and all living things, to actually adore or worship the Source from which it all came seems difficult for those having Freewill. To fully love and admire your Creator should be a daily hour by hour practice, not something reserved for a once-a-week Sunday church meeting and then abandoned the rest of the time or never thought of at all in the currently popular intellectual climates that foster the seeds of disdain. This lack of reverence has sent many civilizations and even universes to their destruction and so it is your nemesis, your enemy, the satanic aspect within yourself to be overcome in your 12th Universe.

"All twelve universes were created by the one Central Being and then assisted by other immense beings of light and by wise and loving energies unknown to most of you on Earth, but selected for their specific talents by the One-Giver-of-Life. This great plan has generally been captained, if you will, by the twelve Sons, or Rays of God who were created from the awesome power your vocabulary cannot describe and your imagination cannot formulate. Under these superlative twelve Rays, a gigantic congregation of Light Workers was selected to manifest the blueprint of God's life forms into matter and, of course, those souls without the light who do not have reverence and respect for what is planned, are never chosen for other opportunity in these spiritual/scientific implementations.

"It is critical for you to recognize God is expressed though the Rays to your planet and you will need to know which Rays you are most influenced by, which you will be drawn towards in particular. All these Rays come from the Creator and can only express to you on Third Dimensional Earth as light broken into the color spectrum you see in the rainbow. You know them as the seven rainbow colors but actually they are facets of God used to influence certain qualities of your beingness. This may be difficult to understand but if you can accept that color in your World has more than just aesthetic value, even your medical profession can use color for healing purposes as did past civilizations on Earth.

"Blue is like a gentle sedative and brings peace, relaxation and pain relief. It is good when overstimulation has occurred. Red has the opposite use. You have many books about this but they are regrettably not believed by most doctors on your planet.

"In addition to your seven colors of the rainbow, the five higher colors, or Rays, those with more luminosity, are scarcely known at all to you, but that which you call silvery, as in moonlight will be appearing more and more in this time, and is the energy to bring you an emphasis on peace and preservation of life. Silver can come as moon glow or as a blend with your other seven colors to provide different nuances and emphasis to the colors you now know. In theAquarian Age there will be great emphasis on colors, or the Rays, since they are aspects of God.

"'The fall', which is spoken about in many religions, occurred because of this exact issue of lack of reverence, love and commitment to the Source-of-All Life.

"You, bj, have been commissioned by the Spiritual Hierarchy to reveal, through the written word, a more detailed history of the Rays and the fact that there are now forty-nine Rays of energy, aspects of God, pouring onto the Earth to assist Humans to wake up and remember their divine natures. Here I would like for you to explain the first twelve Rays, which are most useful to individuals who now may become aware of the Rays.

# 12.

# Ray One:
# Blue Ray of God's Will or Power

Day of Honor: Tuesday
Chakra: Throat
Angel of the First Ray: Archangel Michael
Elohim of the First Ray: Hercules
Hercules' Divine Complement: Lady Amazonia
Chohan of the First Ray: Ascended Master El Morya Khan
Offices: Lord of the First Ray
Chief of the Darjeeling Council of the Great White Brotherhood

The Master El Moya is dedicated to the teaching of esoteric wisdom. With Kuthumi, Serapis Bey, the Master R and Saint Germain, he sponsored the Theosophical Society, the writings of Madame H. P. Blavatsky and Alice A. Bailey and many others. He sponsors serious students of spiritual awareness and intuition. He works closely with those students interested in astrology and numerology. He sponsors many Third Dimensional schools of higher learning, once called "mystery schools. " Although appearing in meditation to be a stern taskmaster with almost no sense of humor, my experience is he has great love and compassion to offer the serious seeker. He does not work long or consistently with those who are inclined to be egotistical or only concerned with intellectual understanding without developing personal faith. He can assist the student to develop faith in God's Will and to grasp a deeper understanding of Universal Law as it relates to Third Dimensional life on Earth. He usually appears to the student in meditation wearing a turban and a robe. His eyes are intense and dark in color; his gaze penetrates through any deception the student has held. Master El Morya teaches the acceptance of personal responsibility and accountability. He teaches the possibility of the embodiment of the Christ Consciousness within each individual and that discipleship to the Creator God is a necessity. In meditation, when sought, he conveys "the quickening" to his students. His teachings include the use of the mantra I AM THAT I AM and belief in the Christ within. He often refers to his students as "chelas" or "adepts. " He is sometimes referred to as Master M. His signature is M.

Ray Colors: Cobalt Blue and White
Gemstones: Sapphire, Lapis Lazuli and Diamonds
Fragrance: Frankincense
Relates to Human Sense: Touch
Constellations: Aries – Leo – Capricorn
Planet: Vulcan
Music: "Pomp and Circumstance", refers to a set of marches by Sir Edward Elgar, also known as "Land of Hope and Glory" (music only) "Onward Christian Soldiers", was adapted from slow movement of Hayden's Symphony No. 53 (music only) when first published as a hymn words by Rev. S. Baring-Gould, tune by J. B. Dykes.

**Purpose and Uses of the First Ray:**
God qualities amplified through the First Ray are Omnipotence and Perfection. It may be invoked for protection. It may be invoked for an individual to have the faith to do the Will of God. The First Ray may be called forth to assist a person to become self-ruled, self-dependent, self-actualized, through understanding the Will of God for their own lives as well as the Divine Plan of the Creator for Earth, this Galaxy and Universe. This is a Ray for developing independence and intuition in order to become self-governed through spiritual awareness and, therefore, free. It gives the power to become one's own authority through spiritual discernment of God's Will. A person infused with the First Ray accepts his own divine nature and a willingness to be his own divine authority, to be self-controlled and to develop self-mastery.

The First Ray virtues are: Truth, Faith and the Will and Power to Create. In order to stay balanced, it is important to balance the drive of the First Ray with the energies of Love and Wisdom, the energies of the Second and Third Rays.

# 13.

# Ray Two: Yellow Ray of Enlightenment – Love – Wisdom

Day of Honor: Sunday
Chakra: Crown
Angel of the Second Ray: Archangel Jophiel
Elohim of the Second Ray: Apollo
Apollo's Divine Complement: Lady Lumina
Chohan of the Second Ray: Ascended Master Lord Lanto
Lord Lanto's Divine Complement: Lady Christine
Offices: Lord of the Second Ray
Master of the Golden Flame of Illumination
Master of the Chinese-green Fire for Precipitation
Member of the Council of Ascended Masters

Lord Lanto teaches the mantra of balance: "I AM Alpha and Omega in the white fire core of Being. " He teaches initiative and action; "rule your circumstances and be not ruled by them". He teaches, "Judge not lest you be judged". He teaches one to be as concerned about the life of others as he is about one's own, the life of karma yoga. He teaches the rearrangement of energies from various octaves, the alchemy of the Holy Spirit. His is a teaching of entering into the flow of the God within. To be the artisan of the Spirit is the goal. He teaches that we have the power and authority to call all circumstances to come into alignment with THE GREAT LAW, the authority to command life. Energy is God. Lord Lanto assists in removing the veils of ignorance, maya. He offers the administration of the fires of understanding to his students. His focus is with the youth of the World.

Ray Colors: Yellow and Gold
Gemstones: Yellow Diamond, Yellow Sapphire and Topaz
Fragrance: Myrrh
Flower: White Fire Lilies
Sense: Hearing
Constellations: Gemini – Virgo – Pisces
Planet: Jupiter
Music: "Song of the Evening Star" from the opera Taunhauser by Wagner
"Chariots of Fire" by Vangelis

**Purpose and Uses of the Second Ray:**
The Second Ray amplifies the three-fold flame of the Cosmic Christ Consciousness, Omniscience, Understanding, Illumination, Perception, Wisdom and Desire to Know God through the Mind. The major focus of the Second Ray is to inspire individuals to turn knowledge into Wisdom and to temper Wisdom with Love and Compassion. The Second Ray represents "feeling-knowledge" and "brotherhood". It also teaches us not to carry altruism to lengths, which are absurd (to the point of weakening the other). It teaches us not to assist others beyond what is to their highest good, whether it is animal or Human. Those students seeking the Love/ Wisdom initiation and balance of their masculine/feminine natures may invoke the Second Ray.

# 14.

# Ray Three: Pink Ray of Divine Love – Active Intelligence

Day of Honor: Monday
Chakra: Heart
Angel of the Third Ray: Archangel Chamuel
Elohim of the Third Ray: Hero
Hero's Divine Complement: Lady Amora
Chohan of the Third Ray: Ascended Master Paul the Venetian
Master Paul the Venetian's Divine Complement: Lady Charity

Offices: Master Paul the Venetian wears a pink cape lined in green. He is a scientist as well as an artist. He tutors his students in the Law of Love and the Law of Discipline. His focus is on art, music, architecture, engineering and the culture of Divine Mother, which antedates Lemuria and goes back to the earliest Golden Ages of Earth. His teaching includes the belief that the more disciplined we are the more energy of Love we can express. He teaches techniques for expressing Love through the creation of beauty, symmetry and design in form, in ritual and the balance of heart, head and hand. "The art of living Love is to be creative. The art of being creative is to be self-disciplined." His teaching focuses on the Cosmic Christ Consciousness, fleur-de-lis, Love, Power and Wisdom. He is devoted to the perfecting of the soul and the development of the intuitive and creative faculties of the heart. His special gift is to teach students the discernment of spirits.

Ray Colors: Pink and Rose
Gemstones: Ruby, Diamond, Garnet, Rose Quartz and Pink Beryl
Fragrance: Rose
Related to Human Sense: Feeling Nature
Constellations: Cancer – Libra – Capricorn
Planet: Saturn
Music: "Brahms' Lullaby" by Johannes Brahms
"Hail Mary Mother of the Flame"
"Music of the Spheres" Stephen Halpern
Music of St. John of the Cross

**Purpose and Uses of the Third Ray:**
The Third Ray amplifies the qualities of Tolerance, Love, Adoration, Discipline, Creativity, Tact, Diplomacy, Arbitration, Patience, Forbearance, Unity, Brotherhood, Culture, Beauty and Perfecting the Manifestation of Heart. The Third Ray is the Ray of the refined mind, the spoken word and abstract intellect – the plane of Spirit and the higher causal mind. This Ray may be called upon when there is a need to discern spirits. The Third Ray strengthens Tolerance, Tact and Patience, and tempers the desire for perfection and intellectual pursuit with common sense and sincerity. Students seeking initiation of The Tree of Life or The Sacred Heart may invoke the Third Ray.

# 15.

# Ray Four: White Ray of Purity (Ray of The Divine Mother) Harmony Through Conflict

Day of Honor: Friday
Chakra: Base of the Spine
Angel of the Fourth Ray: Archangel Gabriel
Elohim of the Fourth Ray: Purity
Purity's Divine Complement: Astrea
Chohan of the Fourth Ray: Ascended Master Serapis Bey
Master Serapis Bey's Divine Complement: Lady Hope
Offices: Lord of the Fourth Ray
Keeper of the Ascension Flame
Member of the Council of Ascended Masters

Master Serapis Bey works with chelas to teach, "Love Is Perfected In Love", the motto above the Ascension Temple. He works with beings that choose to raise their energy vibration in reparation for ascension.

Color: Fiery white with a crystal glow
Gemstones: Diamond, Pearl, Zircon and Quartz Crystal
Fragrances: Lilac and Hyacinth
Flower: Calla Lily (Easter Lily)
Related Human Sense: Sight
Constellations: Taurus – Scorpio – Sagittarius
Planet: Mercury

Music: "Triumphal March" and "Celeste Aida" from Aida "Liebestraum"by
Franz Liszt

**Purpose and Uses of the Fourth Ray:**
The attributes of the Fourth Ray are Purity, Action, Clarity, Discipline,
Intuition, Humility, and Joy. The Fourth Ray is the Ray of Beauty, Harmony,
and Artistic Endeavor, the Ray of Ascension. The Master Serapis Bey says,
"We ascend daily, not all at once. To ascend is to blend in cosmic unity with
the heart of the Eternal. "

The Fourth Ray and its Master brings us in contact with the Feminine
Principle of Creation, the energy of the Divine Mother. The Master says,
"The abundance of every good and perfect, miraculous gift of God is
derived from the white light of the Mother, whose sacred fire breath is at
the heart of every atom and Sun center. "

The Fourth Ray is often called the Ray of "Harmony through Conflict"
or the Ray of struggle. In order to tap into the higher intuitive mind one
must tame the ego and the emotional body, which most often results in
years of struggle and frustration.

The Fourth Ray may be called upon to work miracles and to increase
one's vibrations to move toward ascension. The science of sound and
science of the Word are known in the white fire core of the Fourth Ray.

# 16.

# Ray Five: Green Ray of Truth, Concrete Knowledge and Science

Day of Honor: Wednesday
Chakra: Third Eye
Angel of the Fifth Ray: Archangel Raphael
Elohim of the Fifth Ray: Cyclopea
Cyclopea's Divine Complement: Lady Virginia
Chohan of the Fifth Ray: Ascended Master Hilarion
Master Hilarion's Divine Complement: Mother Mary
Office: Lord of the Fifth Ray, Member of the Council of Ascended Masters

Master Hilarion, together with the Brotherhood of Crete, the Brotherhood of Truth and Pallas Athena, the Goddess of Truth; sponsor teachers of Truth, servants of God, religious leaders and missionaries, as well as those practicing the healing arts, scientists and engineers in all fields, mathematicians, musicians and those specializing in computer and space technology

Master Hilarion is especially concerned with helping atheists, agnostics and skeptics who, because of the leaders of the Church and State, have become disillusioned with religion and life in general. His motto is: "And ye shall know the Truth and the Truth shall make you Free, i. e., Whole. "

Colors: Intense Fiery Green (Emerald-Teal) and Gold
Gemstones: Emerald, Diamond, Jade and Quartz Crystal
Fragrances: Lavender and Peppermint
Related to Human Sense: Inner Vision (Intuition)

Constellations: Leo – Sagittarius – Aquarius
Planet: Venus
Music: "Onward Christian Soldiers", was adapted from slow movement of Hayden's Symphony No. 53 (music only) When first published as a hymn words by Rev. S. Baring-Gould, tune by J. B. Dykes.

**Purpose and Uses of the Fifth Ray:**
Attributes of the Fifth Ray are: Healing, Surrender Selflessness, Concentration, Listening, Dedication, Truth, Science, Precipitation, Actualization, Practicality, Healing, Rejuvenation and Vision. The Fifth Ray is the Ray of Concrete Knowledge and the Mental Plane. One may invoke the Fifth Ray to help strengthen mental focus and to create balance. The Fifth Ray focuses on the scientific attributes of the Laws of Creation and will enhance a person's desire for Truth and Justice. If a person is overly emotional, bringing in the energies of the Fifth Ray will help to create balance.

# 17.

# Ray Six: Ruby Ray of Ministering Grace – Idealism & Devotion

Day of Honor: Thursday
Chakra: Solar Plexus
Angel of the Sixth Ray: Archangel Uriel
Elohim of the Sixth Ray: Peace
Peace's Divine Complement: Aloha
Chohan of the Sixth Ray: Master Lady Nada

As Lord of the Sixth Ray of Ministration and Service, the Ascended Master Lady Nada assists ministers, missionaries, healers, teachers, psychologists, counselors at law, professional people, public servants in government as well as those devoted to serving the needs of God's children in every branch of Human and health services. You will also find her at the side of businessmen and women, blue-collar, skilled and unskilled workers, farmers, and ranchers, defenders of Freedom and revolutionaries of Love in every field. She teaches the principle and practice of sacred labor as the effective means to achieve the goal of ascension.

Offices: Master of the Sixth Ray
World Mother
Member of the Council of Ascended Masters
Member of the Karmic Board
Ray Colors: Purple, Metallic Gold and Ruby
Gemstones: Topaz, Ruby, Alexandrite and Diamond with Pearl
Fragrance: Rose

Related to Human Sense: Speech
Constellations: Virgo – Sagittarius – Pisces
Planet: Neptune
Music: The music of Hildegard of Bingen, "Feather on the Breath of God",
"O Jerusalem"

**Purpose and Uses of the Sixth Ray:**
Virtues of the Sixth Ray are: Devotion, Forgiveness, Healing, Mercy,
Tenderness, Grace, Harmony, Peace and Tranquility. The Sixth Ray is
an emotionally based Ray and one of the purposes of this Ray is to help
dissolve the energies of the lower astral planes. This Ray is focused within
the subconscious mind to endeavor to awaken the subconscious mind to
consciousness. When the subconscious becomes conscious it can then be
in harmony with the superconscious mind. We may invoke the energies
of this Ray to move Humanity out of religious dogma, and a sense of separation, into spiritual awareness and unity consciousness. It can assist in
balancing the masculine and feminine consciousness in individuals and in
the collective of Humanity.

The gifts of the Holy Spirit, which Lady Nada administers, are those of
diverse kinds of tongues and interpretation of tongues. These gifts involve
the mastery of nuances of vibration in the five secret Rays and their almost
infinite combinations with the elements of the seven Rays as the qualities
of the Word are released through the charkas. Lady Nada says, "Therefore,
the Sixth Ray may be invoked to understand diverse kinds of tongues and
the interpretation of tongues. As pertains to Human, divine and Angelic
tongues, these gifts involve the mastery of speech, communication and the
delivery of the Word. They range from the mastery of Earth's languages for
the transmission of the Word universally, to proficiency in the tongues of
Angels, as spoken by the Angelic messengers through the empowerment
of the Holy Spirit. "

Lady Nada is an advocate of children. She may be called upon to assist
in any situation involving children and parenting.

We may invoke the emotional intensity of the Sixth Ray, strengthen it
with the mental focus of the fifth Ray and then blend it with the transfor-
mative energy of the Seventh Ray, and be on our way to mastery.

# 18

# Ray Seven: Violet Ray – Also Known as The Violet Flame of Freedom or Transmutation Ceremonial Magic & Order Alchemy

Day of Honor: Saturday
Chakra: Seat of the Soul
Angel of the Seventh Ray: Archangel Zadkiel
Elohim of the Seventh Ray: Arcturus
Arcturus' Complement: Lady Victoria
Chohan of the Seventh Ray: Ascended Master Saint Germain
Master St. Germain's Divine Complement: Ascended Master Lady Portia
- Goddess of Justice
Offices: Lord of the Seventh Ray
Master of the Violet Flame of Transmutation
Chief of the Council of Ascended Masters
Ray Colors: Violet and Gold
Gemstone: Amethyst
Fragrance: Orchid
Related to Human Sense: Smell
Constellations: Aries – Cancer – Capricorn
Planet: Uranus
Music: "Song of St. Germain", "Hail to the Chief" by James Sanders
"America the Beautiful" words by Katharine Lee Bates, music by Samuel
Agustus Ward, taken from the hymn "Materna" a poem written while Bates

was standing on Pikes Peak, Colorado.

**Purpose and Uses of the Seventh Ray:**
Virtues of the Seventh Ray are: Freedom, Purification, Redemption, Service, Invocation, Manifestation, Diplomacy and Refinement. The Seventh Ray is the Ray of the Aquarian Age. It brings forth the Violet Transmuting flame. It is the Ray of Invocation, manifesting in the highest form of Service. It is the Ray of conscious Transmutation and The Violet Flame is also the Flame of Forgiveness. One may invoke the Angels of the Violet Flame to assist in transforming misqualified energy back into neutral Light Substance and to help move through the transmutation process with ease and grace. The Violet Flame of Transmutation may be called forth to recondition any situation to a state of perfection or homeostasis. It may be invoked to transmute one substance into another, such as lead into gold. It may be invoked to transmute pollution and to promote healing.

INVOCATION OF THE VIOLET RAY

I call upon the Master Saint Germain
I call upon the Elohim Arcturus and Lady Victoria
I call upon the Archangel Zadkiel
Of the Violet Ray
To pour Divine Transmutation
Through all that I AM.

I call upon the Amethyst Ray
To transform every cell,
Every atom of my bodies
Into Higher Light.

I call upon the Violet Flame
To burn within my soul
And to release all veils
That separates me from Spirit.

I call upon the Violet Flame to burn away my illusions,
To burn away my resistances,
And to transmute my fear into love.

So be it.

LORD OF THE SEVEN RAYS:

Office: Lord Maha Chohan, Liberator of the Sacred Fire of All Seven Rays
Days of Honor: All Seven
Chakra: Eighth Chakra
Retreat: Ceylon (Sri Lanka)
Vibration of Colors: White, Pink, Rose, Ruby, White Fire Core Colors of All Rays
Gemstones: Diamond, Yellow Diamond, Topaz, Ruby, Rose Quartz, Pink Beryl and Pearl
Related to Human Quality: Breath of Life
Music: "Ave Maria" (Hail Mary) by Franz Schubert, is a prayer consisting partly of biblical salutations of the Archangel Gabriel and Elizabeth to the Virgin Mary and partly of matter added in the 15th century from Walter Scott's poem "The Lady of the Lake".
Gift: Initiation of the Eighth Chakra

# 19.

# Ray Eight: Aquamarine Ray of Clarity (Transfiguration)

Angel of the Eighth Ray: Angel Rekiaus
Chohans of the Eighth Ray: Lady Nada (World Mother) – Lady Kuan Yin (Goddess of Mercy) – Mother Mary – Lady Claire – Lady Master Venus – Lady Amethyst
Office: Members of Council of the Feminine Power of Creation
Ray Colors: Aqua, Purple and Lavender
Gemstones: Aquamarine, Emeralds, Pearls and Amethyst
Fragrances: Roses and Lavender
Symbol: The Rose
Music: "Colors of the Wind" Elton John
"Candle in the Wind" Elton John and Bernie Taupin
Music of Hildegard of Bingen
"Feather on the Breath of God", "O Jerusalem"
Braham's Lullaby by Johannes Braham

**Purpose and Uses of the Eighth Ray:**
The Eighth Ray amplifies the energy of Nurturing, Compassion, Forgiveness, Consolation, Transformation, Transfiguration, Creation, and Clarity to any person or situation.

## 20.

# Ray Nine: Magenta Ray of Harmony

Angel of the Ninth Ray: Angel Zionnas
Chohan of the Ninth Ray: Ascended Master Lady Kuan Yin, "Goddess of Mercy"
Offices: Master of the Ninth Ray
Member of the Council of Ascended Masters
Member of the Council of the Feminine Power of Creation
Ray Colors: Magenta and Gold
Gemstones: Rubies, Sapphires and Opals
Symbol: Lotus Flower
Fragrances: Sandalwood and Roses
Music: Canon in D with ocean sounds by Johann Pachelbel
Music of Hildegard of Bingen
"Feather on the Breath of God"
"O Jerusalem"

**Purpose and Uses of the Ninth Ray:**
The Ninth Ray may be invoked to call forth Harmony to replace any kind of discord or confusion. The Ninth Ray promotes Clarity.

# 21.

# Ray Ten: Gold Ray of Etrenal Peace

Angel of the Tenth Ray: Angel Gustavius
Chohan of the Tenth Ray: Master Melchizedek
Offices: THE ANCIENT OF DAYS
Chief of Council of THE ANCIENTS
Lord of the Tenth Ray
Priest of the Most High God
Head of the Council of Healers and Ministers
Head of the Order of Melchizedek
Ray Colors: Gold, White and Royal Purple
Gemstones: Gold, Pearls, Diamonds, Amethyst and Moldavite
Fragrances: Cinnamon and Nutmeg
Music: "Messiah" by George Frideric Handel (music only)

**Purpose and Uses of the Tenth Ray:**
The Tenth Ray may be called forth to create peace in any situation.

# 22

# Ray Eleven: Peach Ray of Divine Purpose

Angel of the Eleventh Ray: Angel Ziekius
Chohan of the Eleventh Ray: Master Viracocha
Offices: Lord of the Eleventh Ray, Member of Council of Elders
Ray Colors: Peach and Aqua
Gemstones: Tourmaline and Aquamarine
Fragrances: Hibiscus and Freesia
Music: Peruvian Flute Music

**Purpose and Uses of the Eleventh Ray:**
The Eleventh Ray may be invoked to increase an awakening in Humanity from spiritual amnesia; to awaken Humanity to their own divinity and the truth of the Creator God. This Ray may be invoked to awaken an individual to their soul contract and purpose.

# 23.

# Ray Twelve: Opal Ray of Transformation

Angel of the Twelfth Ray: Angel Merconius
Chohan of the Twelfth Ray: Master Quetzalcoatl
Offices: Lord of the Twelfth Ray
Chief of Council of the Opalescent Rays (Council of Seven)
Ray Colors: Opalescent spectrum of all seven rainbow colors
Gemstones: Diamonds, Watermelon Tourmaline, Opals of all ranges and Moldavite
Fragrances: Hyacinth and Copal incense
Symbols: Plumed Serpent, Butterflies (Swallowtail & Monarch) and Seashells
Music: Flute music of Galoway, "Amazing Grace"
  "Danny Boy" (music only) possibly written by Rory Dall O'Cahan Morison
  "Greensleeves" author unknown (music only)
  "Colors of the Wind" from Pocahontas by Elton John
  "Candle in the Wind" by Elton John
  "Circle of Life" from The Lion King by Elton John
  "How Great 'Thou Art" by Carl G. Boherg, 1885

**Purpose and Uses of the Twelfth Ray:**
The Twelfth Ray may be invoked to bring the energy of Transformation of Human consciousness from religious persecution and slavery to acceptance of diversity and equality of all people as equal and divine.

The Twelfth Ray focuses the energy of the Cosmic Christ Consciousness. Jesus says, "If you would be a true scientist and an understanding

Human being, it is critical for you to recognize God is expressed through the Rays to your planet and you will need to know by which Rays you are most influenced, which you will be drawn towards in particular. Your soul can give you this information.

"All of these Rays come from the Creator and can only express to you on Third Dimensional Earth, as light broken into the color spectrum you see in the rainbow and now as the double rainbow. You have known them as the seven rainbow colors but actually they are facets of God used to influence certain qualities of your beingness. This may be difficult to understand but if you can accept that color in your World has more than just aesthetic value and, personally, you have a responsibility to call them forth for your own use and to enhance Humanity's spiritual growth. I leave you with these thoughts. "

The scientists of this World should realize spiritual power is the basis of what Humans call science.

# 24.

# Jesus Speaks of Military and Governments

"Reverence, love and cooperation with the Spiritual Hierarchy is vital if Humans are to advance spiritually. Many souls on the Earth today have forgotten they are to b the caretakers of the Earth. Without a change of heart they will never gain the power and responsibility in the Aquarian Age to reverse what has happened to Earth. The souls who are now crossing over, out of their bodies, who have done no work toward spiritual growth, will not be allowed to reincarnate upon the Earth. Two planets, Ploarus and Octegon, have been created as remedial schools in the Second and Third Dimension for these souls to begin again; to have an opportunity to remember their own divinity and to trust and believe in God, the Creator of All Things.

"Loving thoughts and sincere respect for all life are necessary at this time to balance the evil active on the Earth. You can help to balance evil through the power of positive belief, positive thoughts, silent reverie, or meditation, during which the Forces of Light will be with you in thought and guidance. Spiritual contemplation is vital now.

"I came long ago physically and I am now available again telepathically to help to bring Human thoughts toward peace and non-violence. Your bodies, your souls, your planet and space itself are all in jeopardy because of some Earthlings' perverted intentions with weaponry and actions of war, hatred and violence.

"I come to point out these current deplorable attitudes and to help overcome the evil thoughts and actions used against others. You are hereby advised and warned if Humanity continues its sickening development of Space Age weaponry, you will have returned to you exactly what you give out. So if your fear, hatred and violence are expressed to others in the Universe, they will return to you in a measure of intense suffering and pain. Why? Because what is given must return. Invent with love, invent with intention to help Humanity and never to harm. I remind you there are Moral Laws required of every soul and you are required to obey these Laws and not to misuse their applications against anyone, anywhere. The scientific community is now advised it cannot just bring evil into existence and disavow any responsibility for its use by what you call government and/or military.

"Your explorers and scientists excuse themselves by saying all they desire is to unlock the secrets of the Universe. They have no understanding of the truth of the Universe and the other occupants. How would a government and its military personnel take bombs or killer satellites or particle beams and employ them against other life forms if Humans refused to create them or utilize them? Governments and military are run by Humans. Humans are the ones making these choices. They are making these choices without ever thinking of God or the Earth or other civilizations.

"I warn those of you who are creating these weapons for killing you must accept full responsibility for your actions. This is true whether a person is hired with research funds by government aid or by funds of so-called non-military organizations. It is true whether you are in or out of uniform. The responsibility cannot be shifted with a shrug of the shoulders and the thought that someone else bears that responsibility. Be advised if you continue in this madness you will bear responsibility for its result.

"You Humans of Earth are not all of God's handiwork. You are a blink in the vast network of life that stretches far beyond the light of your own Milky Way galaxy. I remind you that you are suburban dwellers of an enormous, magnificent light and life creation. Treat all of it with the dignity, love and respect due it and you will be permitted to advance into the higher dimensions where life truly resides. You are not alone in this vast consciousness called space. Each act you perform, each thought you express, is carried along the Network of Light you are unable to see. What you send out returns, but also affects other along the way.

"Space is not empty, nor is it to be abused. It is not a dumping ground or an area you can claim as yours. All belongs to God and you are merely custodians of it, even as you were given dominion, or custodianship of the planet Earth long eons ago. What have you done with that responsibility? Are you so proud of its condition and the kind of life you've created here that you wish to share it with other life forms?

" You volunteered as caretakers of Earth and have been evaluated as unsuited to further tasks until that one is satisfied and then you may be worthy to carry its value forward to other consciousnesses. Clean up your minds and hearts and the ground on which you walk. Then you will be a fit companion to other life forms who already exist and have been watching your violent nature with the suspicion it deserves for many years. Mentally superior beings have always monitored your life behaviors, in constant surveillance of what Earth Humans are doing, especially in the ever growing insanity of your space race and invention of advanced weaponry. Since the atomic bomb they have been particularly positioned around the Earth to assure protection to space and the life forms in it, but they have watched for thousands of years.

"Unless you heed God's warning and come to a state of love on Earth, with the help of those here in the heavenly realms, you are considered detrimental to life and will be treated accordingly if there are further transgressions made. We, your teachers of Light and Love, have come again to warn you. We suggest some specific actions that are now required if you intend to save your bodies, your souls, your beautiful planet and the space beyond your tiny speck of life.

"You may not violate the space lying beyond the 250-mile strip of your own boundaries with weaponry. You may not take weapons into space without the Creator's permission. The reason is simple. If your intentions are not loving, you are morally diseased and unfit to do so. In a sense, you are as contagious, as your violent thoughts and actions demonstrate to the greater family beyond your borders. You are, as of now, quarantined until further notice. Open your minds and hearts to the love of God; change your behavior, live in peace.

"There are presently madmen in many countries working on weapons. Underground hydrogen explosions in both Russia and the United States are likely, and there are a myriad of other experiments with killer satellites, particle beams and other offensive weapons currently in use already. These will not be tolerated any longer. Hydrogen is an elemental building block of the Universe and must not be harmfully employed in any way at any time. Hydrogen explosions could affect the entire Universe.

"You must cease offensive space launchings until you become morally acceptable life-mates to the other beings who watch you now. We of the spiritual realms will be powerless to aid you if you continue in this madness. You will have taken the matter out of our hands and space will be defended against your insanity. Any grace I brought 2000 years ago cannot save you from the Cause and Effect principle after this warning because of the present and potential damage you are causing.

"Cease planning, constructing, or employing any space weaponry immediately. You cannot hide behind statements like 'The government is doing it or it's the military.' All of Humanity is responsible in one way or another. You cannot hide behind the evil of war on your planet and say you have no relationship to it. You must turn your attention to peace and find a way to make peace profitable. When peace, not war. is profitable and desirable there will be a great practice of love and sharing which your God has taught you. Those who promote war and those who make no effort on the behalf of peace on this planet are not accepting the guardianship role which has been given to Humanity. You are the caretakers of the Earth and all life upon it. This is your destiny and your purpose.

"Know that you are at a critical moment in Earth's history and evolution. You must stop believing that there is evil in every Human heart and that one nation is out to destroy all others. Without a belief in peace you will behave with suspicion, hatred and vengeance. Stop now and remember love and forgiveness are your only helpmates in achieving planetary peace. Who among your so-called Christian countries will put my teachings into practice as the way forward?

"The so-called primitives whom you self-righteously seek to civilize were closer to God's mission than you with your massive technology turned against Humanity's good. Have they assaulted space and the invisible life beyond your own boundaries? What does being civilized mean? How do you describe Earth today? Is it a civilized planet to be emulated?

"Because you are frightened men and women you only have frightened nations, separate from one another. What lies within each one of you, in-dividually, is projected into the larger global connection you think of as Earth. You have forgotten what peace is. Because you have forgotten what peace is, many spiritual teachers have come to Earth, with repetitive regu-larity to remind you to challenge your soul's recollection, to reinstate you in the Father/Mother flock. Yet through willful disobedience and stubborn resistance to love, this beautiful planet Earth is now in jeopardy from the very ones she has fed and persistently nurtured.

"Long ago, when you lived in a Spirit form, there was only one govern-ment in heaven, that government was God, which is love. When you fell away from constancy of that one love mind and separated into the physical body form now used on Earth, your challenge, your responsibility, was to rejoin that former belief and evolve back to that which you had experienced before. In this emergence you would have chosen God above all things. If you did this, you would be a useful member of a vast and marvelous Universe strewn with planetary bodies, star systems and a myriad of life forms. We smile at your concept of heaven as a quiet harp-playing existence. There is peace here, and there is music, but it is not at all dull or boring, I promise you. Great activity and adventure exist for those who are able to share their heart love and apply God's wisdom and direction.

"A choice for or against God must be made; a choice for peace or war. If all or most of you choose God and peace, the planet will not have to be cleansed and will rise as a beacon of light in the Universe as an example for other life forms. If only a majority learn this required lesson, then only the majority will be allowed soul progress as examples for others to observe and emulate.

"I came years ago to share this message and prepare you to cleanse your soul of false beliefs. I come again to remind you that time is running short. The concept of peace awaits personal and planetary application. Only your belief that you can be harmed allows such things as weapons in the first place. It is your soul's growth which is vital. Your American money says 'In God we trust' and your pledge of allegiance states America is 'One nation under God,' but what you profess is not how you live. Your only choice is whether you can let go of fear long enough to change your own behavior and all of your countries governments' view of life and then seek love and peace as an ultimate reality.

"What will happen depends very much on the plans and activities of your governments. So keep love in your heart and radiate great light and insist your government take actions for the people's goal of peace. If half of every nation's population were absolutely focused on peace, life on this planet would change. Peace is a powerful belief and for Humanity on Earth it is now a necessity.

"To all government officials, elected or autocratically empowered and to all military leaders on this planet, from generals down to the lowest private in any military force, I speak bluntly. War is the opposite of peace. It is not based on love, but rather on the deliberate destruction of other Human lives. Those battles of one nation against another are inherently wrong because all of Humanity is created by God. If you deliberately plan a war, and attack others, you are creating for your soul a terrible effect which you will have to repay at a later time. I therefore caution you not to kill or destroy any life form.

"Earth and Humanity are being observed. If any nation on Earth makes further serious moves of violence or threat into the ether beyond Earth's boundaries, you will likely be contained in some fashion. Do not enter space on anything but an unarmed, peaceful mission, certainly not with created weaponry, which will violate God's inter-federation boundaries and agreements.

"Meanwhile, for the Light Workers of Humanity known to me and other World teachers in the spiritual realm, be comforted to know that through your daily meditation you will be personally informed of what is occurring so you will always be exactly where you should be for your soul's purpose. You need to commune with the soul part of you which knows what you should do for the greater good. Through your meditation practice you can send love from your heart to this beautiful Earth and to all those negative forces which seek power, war and violence. Remember a great mental force created heaven and Earth and all the Universes. Use your own mental love energies to assist us now in reclaiming your planet Earth for God. Anger may give initial impetus to a cause, but it causes division and separateness if maintained. Wake up from your spiritual amnesia. "

# 25.

# Jesus Speaks to Parents and Teachers

"Beginning in the last couple of decade's children who are old souls came with an eagerness to express God's love, to grow in light and understanding, and to populate the planet preparing it for the thousand years of peace.

"Every Human is a teacher merely by their presence on the planet. Be careful what you model and exemplify because actions speak louder than words; they speak a universal language. Your soul answer regarding parenting and teaching will have different replies than those made by your lower personality, which may be interested in parenting to please families or because it is what people always do or because teaching is simply a way to earn money. The soul's answer lies beyond these reasons for its need is to experience God's love and return it to all living creatures. There is also a deep desire to learn and grow.

"As a parent, above all, be ready for the unusual. At this time in spiritual evolution be flexible and know you will magnetize a soul which needs to be approved and supported for its ability to see beyond earthly definitions.

"Take these suggestions to heart and as you apply them there will be great personal joy and delight as you practice God's love and exuberance. Although there is responsibility in this, let it not become the somber dutifulness that has choked off the message I brought before. Do these things cheerfully. Important tasks done well can give both responsibility and joy. Remember this, lighten up in your outlook. The new children will teach you this joy from their personal experience with invisible realms which I once came to share. Heaven is a joyful state of learning and sharing and loving. To think less than this is to misunderstand it totally.

"The purpose and promise of this Golden Age is to fill the Earth with beings of a nurturing, loving nature whose devotion to God sends out a Blaze of Light vibrations dancing like rainbows and sunlight embracing the entire globe.

"Understand some of these small Golden Age beings, with great soul knowledge and awareness, started arriving a couple of decades or so ago. Others are coming now and more will be arriving soon. Many of them may outshine your own abilities to see and hear the spiritual beings like myself. They may have mental capabilities you lack. Mind over matter will become the new reality. Therefore, your first step is to accept that although you are the bigger in body you may not be spiritually wiser. For the personalities of some parents this will be a great blow to Human pride. But the parents' souls will rejoice for the experience of psycho-spiritual abilities will be a major part of the New Age life.

"As a parent, teacher or grandparent, do not let your pride get in the way if you see the little ones talking to invisible Angels or hearing inner heavenly voices. Many grandparents will be raising their grandchildren during this Age. I assure you, as a child, you had more of that ability than you have now. The reason you lost it was the adults around you had forgotten these abilities themselves because of parental, societal and educational displeasure or ridicule of some kind. Many children in your own generation heard and saw the Angelic realms, but were forced to abandon this ability because they could not face a loss of respect and love from family, friends or teachers who denied this reality.

"You must acknowledge the children's abilities to both the children and others and do not ridicule or deny their connections with the heavenly realms which are very real to them and which will become more real to you both if you allow and encourage this communication. In fact, if you are willing to grow from your interactions with the children, you will learn as much or more than you teach.

"My greatest suggestion for all Humanity, especially you as parents and teachers, is to say something like, 'until now' or 'we have believed until now...' For instance, if teaching science to a child say, 'Up until now we have believed the speed of light of 186,000 miles per second is the fastest travel possible. Look within and see if this sounds right to you.' In other words, give present knowledge the tentative nature it deserves, for, in fact, this is not a correct way of looking at the speed of light. The wise ones beyond the veil will be working with the incarnated ones to correct much erroneous material that passes on Earth as accurate, not just about nature and the

Universe, but also about the *Bible*.

"Not only are the Angels and Ascended Masters willing to teach the little ones, they are willing, by the process of mental telepathy, to teach you more of the truth of the Universe and your place in it, as well. However, to pierce the veil, you must believe it is possible, you must become very quiet and still in order to hear the truth, and you must be grateful for the Divine Plan that God has given Humankind. Meditation will help.

"Once, eons ago, you lived only in God's mind and all things were known to you. After decent into materiality, you were no longer connected in the same way. You became, in a very real sense, lost in space without your communication device. Fortunately, we who love you and seek to restore your connectedness back to God, so that the division between heaven and Earth is joined and then you can once again be part of God's love and knowledge.

"Humanity's fall, or detour out of communication and direct awareness of all that is known to the Creator, is being revived for you if you wish to have it restored. This is the truth, but you must be willing, of your own Freewill, to accept and joyously participate in its restoration. Like a broken television or radio set, let yourself be repaired to receive the heavenly channels that await you once more. Or at least attune yourself exactly in a clear state of reception.

"I, The Christ, am not the only channel of God's truth. There are many others. But for those who believe and have faith in me, I assure you that I am no farther away, once you restore your communication system, than a mental phone call. One day soon many more will actually see me than do now, especially the children.

"You were told in the *Bible* you needed to become like a little child. I meant by this you must have no limitations in your thinking. No barriers that say, 'Oh, that's not possible.' And like a child, you must be accepting of a loving Father/Mother's role in your life. Not a parent who would be unworthy of trust or would abuse you, but one whose affection and concern are eternal and assured. TRUST IS THE BASIS OF LOVE.

"It is not I who has created the plan. However, it is I, and others in heaven, who have totally accepted and participated in it. Your task is the same. For the sake of the Golden Age children, you should encourage them to experience contact with what you may not yet see and hear yourself. This will mean surrendering the past ideas you were taught and to be ever present in the moment. Spiritual evolution is accelerating to bring you home again to heaven. Build your own communication lines through meditation and encourage every person you know to do the same.

"Children are open, curious and willing to love, to learn. Be like a child so you can be taught. You will feel the peace and harmony and love for which your soul yearns.

"Teachers are faced with an almost superhuman challenge in the present educational system since, in most cases, their textbooks are partially distorted, incomplete, or untrue and in many systems no textbooks are now given. Children are expected to use computers and the Internet to research information and most of the information given there is only people's opinions and not the truth, especially about history. School organizations and boards have established curricula that society requires as manuals of truth. These are study guides of agreements about what is true on Earth; however, these generally limit the heart and mind. As teachers, do not give present information as truth or you fail in your soul's task as an opener of Human consciousness.

"Tell the children and adults that, until now, these are the ideas Humankind has believed, but always ask them to go deeply within to see if they feel these ideas are true. Be willing to allow freedom of expression and new ideas. Always suggest, 'This is what we've always thought, but what if there is more to know? What would it be?'

"The primary attitude is not to be dogmatic out of your own need for security. Be willing to know more yourself. If science is your field, be open to new discoveries and applications; be willing to receive previously unseen connections of truth. In your meditations ask to be made a gifted teacher of these new beings and ask to continually deepen the truth of whatever subjects you teach. You will be absolutely assisted if your motive is love and peace your goal.

"By mental telepathy a few of you may even talk with the great teachers of the past to see how they would update their Earth teachings given that opportunity. Be open to the expanded Universe that will whisper its secrets to those minds willing to receive. Be a model of turning within and your children will feel safe turning within.

"Many social and educational beliefs must fall. Welcome change; accept a greater understanding. Children need encouragement, support and your love. Many will be masters of truth, heralds of this coming Golden Age, who need unique nurturing. Until now your schools have filled students with your facts, many of which are false. We put no blame on educators, but challenge their self-evaluation. We suggest teaching that Humans must tune within to know the truth of all things.

"Many of these incoming children arriving now are of a higher vibration in energy than most parents who give them physical birth. They may be more spiritually capable than most of their teachers on Earth. Your first step as a teacher or parent needs to be to acknowledge their capabilities make you no less. In fact, it offers you the greatest opportunity of your life. Do not be defensive; be curious. Encourage openness.

"All children are closer to God when they arrive than are adults who live in cultural conditioning which forces much of their true nature underground. Each generation will arrive in higher vibration than the one preceding. Help the children to be all they are and can become.

"God is not static. You are not static. Change is ever present and necessary. Our Father/Mother God is, indeed, magnanimous and generous to all, but you must be willing to receive the truth. Open your mind and heart to receive your own abundance of truth.

"In your teaching you are blessed for you join the work that I, The Christ, and many other spiritual teachers came to do. Let us be partners in God's plan for bringing the Human family back to the heavenly dimension that is its destiny. There are many ways these lessons of looking within can be taught without the use of the word 'God.' Words such as Light or Source and Oneness can mean many things, as can words such as intuition, the inner knower, or the truth bringer. The Creator does not care what name is used.

"A few of you will truly change the organizational structure, content and usefulness of education. But whatever your parts, large or small, play it with love and dedication and you cannot fail. By listening within, you will always be guided to the highest good and finest choices. Teach the children quiet times are essential and will provide them with strength, certainty and inner knowing.

"Parents and grandparents have the greatest opportunity to teach and model the New Age awareness to children because of proximity. Teaching your children who they truly are and giving them the encouragement to take leadership where their soul would have them go is a valid task in this time.

"Mothers, you are not just producing babies. You are bringing forth the life form a soul needs for purposes of growth, love and service. Talk to the soul of the babe while it is yet in the womb and discuss with it what purpose it wishes to express upon the planet. Remember always the child is not your property or possession. It belongs to God and to all that exists beyond your tiny experience. Do not limit the being as you share a code of spiritual responsibility and joyous love.

"Before the pregnancy you must cleanse yourselves of as much doubt and limitation as possible and as a couple pray together you will rise fully to this great occasion of child rearing. Listen to what your soul and higher guidance advises you to do in this process of providing a physical body for another soul to use on its earthly journey.

"Birth brings a soul its greatest trauma for it is cut off from its usual place in the light, the joy and peace. It often becomes sad or depressed at the surroundings it finds on Earth. Provide a tone of caring long before it enters life and continue that attitude throughout the years you have offered to be responsible for this soul's visitation. Give structure of loving responsibility for the child's welfare. This does not mean letting the child's personality do as it wishes, for the Human personality has to cooperate with its soul through willingness and understanding. It must learn to respect the rights of others. Many of the higher level beings choosing to enter Humanity at this time do not wish to come in through the trauma of the birth canal. They are choosing to come through cesarean sections and some are by passing the birth process and walking in to adult bodies rather than living through puberty and adolescence.

"This is true of every adult personality on Earth, not just the children. When an adult is asked to surrender to God it does not mean become a vegetable without purpose or goals. It means the little Human personality becomes viable and useful to the soul without the fears and anxieties, guilts and uncertainties that plague an individual's habits, habits created by those early conditionings and personality tendencies.

"Humanity's goal is to produce as few of these negative conditionings and limited beliefs in each child as possible. These are the barriers and misqualified thoughts will have to be acted out and released later in order for the soul to focus its full expression and delight into the body which is its physical form here on Earth. To create an open space for the soul to practice truth and love is the main purpose of the physical body experience.

"Telling a child the basic belief that God is a loving and unlimited Source is obviously far more important than saying we are sinners and that God will punish us for our sins. God does not punish us. The Law of Karma repays us for our thoughts and actions. The fewer false beliefs you fill a child with the less cleansing she/he will have to let go later. I continue to be saddened and appalled at the ideas your churches' program into the minds of children and adults to frighten them and dishearten them. These ideas describe a God whose nature is fearsome and capricious, at best. Who could love such a God?

"Our Creator is not like this fearsome, heavy-handed, punishing figure taught by many religions today. Teach your children the truth and do not let such nonsense fill their subconscious minds with this evil. These teachings have sabotaged the love and forgiveness message I brought 2,000 years ago. I am grieved my meaning could have been so abused and twisted by the ignoble goals of church officials, grieved the masses should believe God held them in such low esteem.

"Our Creator knows nothing but love. The unloving conditions on the Earth come from Humankind. My role was to clarify this truth and help you understand your own thoughts and actions are the bringers of your experience, even when it seems you are not responsible. You are not victims. You are doing it to yourselves. This lesson is what you must teach the children. As co-creators you are responsible for most of life's experiences. Learn this lesson well. Then you can teach it with feeling. Your thought has created the experiences you've had and our effort is dedicated to cleanse your mental and emotional nature so your thoughts are only of love and peace which will return to you.

"Remember my resurrection demonstrated the power of my mind over life and death. Use the power of your own mind for your own resurrection. Please teach the children they are lovable and that the way they think will create their view of life and reality. Tell them God is not some arbitrary old man sitting on a cloud dumping these evil events onto Humankind. Humankind's thoughts have created the condition as they are on Earth now.

"If people are suffering and experiencing difficult times because of persistent negativity of thought, it is not God's doing. This difficulty is self-created, Humanity's creation. When children grow up knowing the truth, there will be a greater opportunity for peace.

"When you and the rest of Humanity can be so cleansed of the Human personalities of fear and the desires for power and control over other people, of the violence and hatred and war, then the circumstances in your times and upon the planet will change. That is why I say unto you the time has come when all must choose God. The higher realms have programmed a heavenly chapter to come now in Earth's history, and this chapter requires positive thinkers. This is your opportunity to believe, live and teach positive thinking.

"Never mind the forecasts of what may happen on the planet so long as you are tuned in daily to your higher self. Accept you will experience only what your soul requires to enter the Golden Age. Fear has no place in the New Age. This is the point of my message. Love is more powerful than all the fear that exists anywhere in the Universe. Teach your children to love and trust God and not to judge themselves or others. Loving, focused thoughts will carry you through any difficulty. That was my message to you long ago and that is still God's goal for you.

"God's presence does not just descend upon Humanity as some external force, but lives within each person as well. God is an intuitive experience, very personal and totally available. My life was a statement that no matter what others said and did (governments, religions, or uniformed people) they could not defeat or change the power of my internal awareness of God.

"My purpose was to show you that even though I was arrested, persecuted and, in the final analysis, abandoned by even my dearest friends and disciples, I knew something more profound than the external physical experience. I knew God. Trust is the cornerstone of love. Teach it to the children.

"You and the children are the seed of God. Within you is the outpouring of the vision which can be denied or ignored but never destroyed. I came to remind you of your identity. I came to say you and the children are a marvelous creation of mind in matter and you can do almost anything you set your minds to. This internal God self is the director of your experience if you would choose it. All children are to be taught kindness and love by your example.

"Tell the children God is present everywhere. In concert with others you are the mind of god present here on the Earth. Accept that responsibility. You are not victims of a malevolent God, not the stepchildren of some angry, raving parent. You have the same potential qualities of love within you that were the Creator's tools in creating the cosmos and the vast regions of space. You have your own mind and your own word with which to create.

"Television is not an adequate babysitter. Most programs are not fit company for adults, let alone children. Be selective in what you give other people permission to put into your children's subconscious memory storage. You are charged with the responsibility of filling the child's 'at home' hours with only the finest conversation, entertainment and live activities. A word of caution about Sunday schools-some Sunday school teachers often used to threaten children by saying 'God will punish you if you are bad.' What must be taught is Human responsibility. When Humans act unloving to themselves and others there will be pain as a reminder that love is not present, this does not come from God it is a result of Universal

Law. God does not punish. A Human's misuse of the Law of Love and also the Law of Cause and Effect harms you.

"One person joined by another, in a growing decision for PEACE, will form an indestructible belief pattern of such magnitude the broader body of power and execution of policy will reflect it. Nothing short of this will save the planet. Become the peace, teach peace and join together in a mighty demand for peace at every level of local, national and international government.

"This Age is energetically lighter and finer in its vibration. From this new higher energy vibration we of the heavens now send you are able to receive the result of your own thoughts more quickly. You will soon think a thought and see its result in your own body or life experience quickly.

"Share with the children that Jesus did not die in his inner self of being, and neither can you, except by the misuse of power. By a person's limited attitudes they can become spiritually retarded. My resurrection was possible because of the love power of my mind over external circumstances, over the belief that death exists. Teach them that I still live and still watch over them and care for them.